FOCUS ON

Advanced English

C·A·E Practice Tests with Guidance

SUE O'CONNELL

Nelson

Thomas Nelson and Sons Ltd
Nelson House Mayfield Road
Walton-on-Thames Surrey
KT12 5PL   UK

51 York Place
Edinburgh
EH1 3JD   UK

Thomas Nelson (Hong Kong) Ltd
Toppan Building 10/F
22A Westlands Road
Quarry Bay Hong Kong

©Sue O'Connell 1993

First published by Thomas Nelson and Sons Ltd 1993

ISBN 0-17-556442-6
NPN 9 8 7 6 5 4 3 2 1

Special thanks go to my friend Sue Scott, of Brunel College, Bristol, for her invaluable comments and suggestions.

The author and publishers would also like to thank the following people who arranged the piloting of material and provided very helpful feedback:

Christopher Hare (Filton College, Bristol), Nic Humphries (The Frances King School of English), Katie Jennings (The Language Centre of Ireland). Glynn Jones and Simon Williams (International House, London). Thanks are also due to those who helped with the recordings: Mary Dallas, Brian Janes, Clare McDowell, Brent Merrylees, Peter and Linda Newberry, Ian Scott, Julia Simnett.

Publishers' Acknowledgements

The publishers would like to thank the following for permission to reproduce copyright material. They have tried to contact all copyright holders, but in cases where they have failed will be pleased to make the necessary arrangements at the first opportunity.

Texts
UCLES for the assessment criteria on which pages 11 and 22 are based; David Thomas for the article 'Look Daddy I can Fly' (page 29); Philippa Davis for the article 'Secrets of Talking Your Way to the Top' (page 30); Rodney Hobson for the article 'Job Seekers ill-suited for Interviews' (page 32); Nick Hanna for the article 'In search of the fish with the longest name' (page 34); Christopher Matthew and *High Life* for the extract from 'Olympic Gold' (page 39); *The Sunday Express* for the extract 'The Big Sleep' (page 40) and Migraine Headaches (page 42); *World Wide Fund for Nature* for the leaflet 'Extinct' (page 50); Paul Bray for the article 'Is the office fit for the job?' (page 53); Karen Jamieson, *This is Bristol and Bath* for the text 'Back-chat' (page 54); *Friends of the Earth*, Peter Butler, J.P. Chambers, Melissa Hawes, S. Charles Lewsen, Judith Pentreath, Richard Pearson, Peggy Harbridge, D.W. Wilcox for their letters on pages 55 and 56; Lorna Siggins, *Cara* Magazine, for the extract 'Oscar's Winning Performance'; Helen Fielding and *The Independent* for the extract 'Cause for Alarm?' (page 61); Mike Hamer and *New Internationalist* for the extract 'Car Chaos' (page 64); Patricia Fenn and *The Sunday Times* for the article 'Cruising' (page 72); Robin Eggar and *The Sunday Mirror* for the text 'Prince of Wales' (page 75); David Tytler and *The Times* for the article 'Classrooms with the writing on the wall' (page 76); Jane Bidder for the article 'How to win prizes for keeping quiet' (page 79); Lusanda Kurukulasariya and *New Internationlist* for the extract 'Talking Rubbish' (page 83); John McManus, *The Irish Times*, for the extract 'New £20 note to prevent forgeries' (page 82); *Carnell Ltd.* for the advertisement 'Travel Free as an Air Courier' (page 83); Charles Bremmer and *The Times* for the extract 'Book reading a lost art at Harvard' (page 86); *Bristol Visitors' Guide* for the extracts from 'Historic Harbour, St. Augustine's Reach' (page 89); *Good Housekeeping Magazine* for the recipe 'Tomato and Artichoke Salad with Basil' (page 90); Susan Hill for the article 'How to find out about dinosaurs' (page 95); Martin Knights for the extract 'Healthier way of life underground' (page 97); Liz Gill and *The Times* for the article 'Curing the ill-mannered' (page 99); Edward Welsh and *The Sunday Times* for the article 'Looking for the special agents' (pages 100/1)' Robin Young and *The Times* for the extract 'Hotels pick up bills for five-star thieves' (page 103); 'Forest Fires' (page 106) adapted from an article in *Paradise Lost*, published by *Earthlife*, in association with the *Observer*; Amy Goldstein at *The Washington Post* for the extract 'Flu Takes Area by Storm' (page 107); Richard Dawood and Oxford University Press for the preface from 'Travellers' Health' (page 109); *The Home Office* for the leaflet 'How to Choose and Use Fire Extinguishers for the Home' (page 118); Karen Gold and *The Independent* for the article 'High-tech practice as the tutor preaches' (page 122); *The Sydney Morning Herald* for the extract 'Why Western Australia's Aborigines are speaking Portuguese' (page 123); Tim Rayment, Philip Beresford and *The Sunday Times* for the article 'Service without a smile' (page 125); *New Internationalist* for the extract 'Flying Pigeons Forever (page 128); *Focus* magazine for the extract 'Ski-ing at the limits' (page 129); Flora Hunter and *The Evening Standard* and Solo Syndication for the extract 'How to have a baby and save your career' (page 130); *Focus* magazine for the extract 'Adapting to the climate – cold comforts and hot sweats' (page 131); Wilson, Etchels and Tulloh and Virgin Publishing for the extracts from *The Marathon Book*.

Photographs
Aerofilms page 143; John Batt pages 137, 138; Chatto and Windus/Caroline Davidson pages 143, 147; Bruce Coleman Ltd page 148; Colour Library Books/Roger Hicks page 143; Thames and Hudson pages 137, 138; Innovations pages 55, 144; Magnum Photos/Martin Parr pages 141, 146; NHPA page 148; Reed Consumer Books Photo Library page 139; Tony Stone Worldwide page 32; The Quiller Press/John Prizeman pages 145, 146.

Illustrations
Joe/Times Newspapers page 27; Benedek/New Internationalist page 62; Bristol City Council page 87; Home Office Publications pages 109, 110; Gary Cook/The Sunday Times page 123.

David Cook, Nick Hardcastle, Robert Kettel, Robert Goldsmith, Kim Lane, Trevor Ridley, Angela Wood.

CONTENTS

INTRODUCTION

About this book

The aim of this book is to help you prepare as effectively as possible for the **Cambridge Certificate in Advanced English (CAE)**, and it is designed to be useful whether are studying alone or attending a class. It includes five complete practice tests, modelled on the most recent CAE exams, and also provides an introduction to the exam and helpful advice on tackling each paper.

Test 1 is a guided test. This means that each of the five papers is introduced and explained, section by section, before you attempt it yourself. You are given examples of the main question types that you can expect to meet together with guidance on answering them. To help you further, there is an Answer Key to Test One on page 47.

Tests 2 and **3** have notes in the page margins to remind you of important points. These will help you to answer the questions and encourage you to approach the exam in the right way.

Tests 4 and **5** are exactly like real examination papers, with no guidance or reminders.

The material in this book has been chosen to represent the widest possible range of topics and styles and also to reflect the emphasis on authenticity in the CAE exam. Reading texts are mostly reproduced in their original format and, in keeping with Cambridge policy, the listening texts include a proportion of authentic recordings and a variety of accents.

Important: To get the most benefit from this book, work carefully through Test 1 to begin with, making sure you are familiar with the requirements of each paper. Only then should you go on to the other tests.

About the CAE exam

If you really want to pass an exam, it's important to know as much about the exam as possible. In this way you find out what to expect from the exam and, more importantly, what the examiners expect from you! This section will help you to increase your knowledge of the CAE and will answer many of the questions which students often want to ask when approaching the exam for the first time.

To see how well-informed you are about the CAE, try answering the short quiz below. You will find the answers when you read the information which follows.

How much do you know about CAE?

1 The level of the exam is halfway between First Certificate and Proficiency.   True ☐   False ☐

2 Each paper is worth 20% of the total marks.   True ☐   False ☐

3 You have to write your answers on a special answer sheet for

   Paper 1 Reading ☐   Paper 2 Writing ☐   Paper 3 English in Use ☐   Paper 4 Listening ☐

4 There is more reading in CAE than in the Proficiency exam.   True ☐   False ☐

5 Paper 1 includes multiple-choice vocabulary questions.   True ☐   False ☐

6 You have to produce two pieces of writing in Paper 2.   True ☐   False ☐

7 You can choose to answer questions on set books in Paper 2.   True ☐   False ☐

8 Paper 3 includes a question where you have to correct grammar mistakes.   True ☐   False ☐

9 In Paper 4, all the recordings are played twice.   True ☐   False ☐

10 For Paper 5, you may be examined individually or with another candidate.   True ☐   False ☐

Let's look at some of the typical questions which candidates ask about the CAE examination.

What level of English do I need for CAE?

The CAE is an **advanced level** exam and it is described by Cambridge as being two thirds of the way between First Certificate and Proficiency. Someone taking CAE therefore needs a good level of ability in the four language skills, listening, speaking, reading and writing and a good grasp of the main areas of grammar. But it is a practical rather than an academic exam and you will not need to deal with literary texts or understand very advanced or specialised vocabulary.

It's worth noting that there is a lot of reading to do in CAE (the texts in the Reading paper amount to approximately 3,000 words, compared with only 1,800 in the Proficiency exam) so you will need to be a confident and efficient reader.

Who is it suitable for?

The CAE exam is designed as a high-level final qualification with an emphasis on real world, practical tasks and it is therefore suitable for people who want to use English in their jobs. It can also serve as a 'stepping-stone' for people who want to develop the language skills necessary for the Proficiency exam.

The CAE is quite a new exam but it is rapidly becoming recognised as an important qualification by employers and educational institutions throughout the world.

What does CAE consist of?

These are the details of the five papers:

Paper 1 Reading 1 hour 15 minutes	There are four texts and approximately 50 questions which test different reading skills. Questions include various kinds of matching, gap-filling and multiple-choice items. There are no multiple-choice vocabulary questions.
Paper 2 Writing 2 hours	Two tasks of approximately 250 words each are set. The first is compulsory, the second is selected from a choice of four topics.
Paper 3 English in Use 1 hour 30 minutes	There are three sections and approximately 70 questions. *Section A* concentrates on the correct choice of grammar and vocabulary. *Section B* tests the ability to correct mistakes and to adapt a text in a particular style. *Section C* tests the ability to organise written English appropriately.
Paper 4 Listening approx. 45 minutes	There are four sections and approximately 45 questions which test a range of listening skills. One of the recordings is heard only once. Questions include various kinds of matching, completion and multiple-choice items.
Paper 5 Speaking 15 minutes	Candidates are examined in pairs by two examiners and there are four phases designed to test a wide range of speaking skills.

Notes: 1 For Papers 1, 3 and 4, the answers must be written on special answer sheets.
       2 There are no set books or optional papers.

How many people take CAE every year? And how many of them pass?

CAE was only introduced world-wide in 1992 and the number of candidates in that first year was about 14,000. This number is expected to increase quickly in coming years. There are 750 examination centres throughout the world and candidates can enter in 60 different countries.

The percentage of those who pass will vary each year, of course, but on average around 65–70% of those who take the exam can expect to pass it.

How many marks do I need to pass CAE?

There is no set pass mark but you would normally be expected to get about 60% in order to pass at Grade C. To allow for slight differences in the difficulty of the exam, the examiners only set the exact level needed for a Pass after the papers have been taken.

Are all the papers equally important?

Yes. Each paper carries 20% of the marks. So, even though the Listening and Speaking papers are much shorter than the written papers, they are worth the same number of marks.

Is it necessary to pass every paper?

No. There are five papers and what counts is your overall score. So it's possible to fail a paper but still pass the exam as a whole if you do exceptionally well on the other papers. But you must sit all of the papers – being absent from any of the papers will automatically mean that you have to take the whole exam again at a future date.

How is the exam graded?

There are three Pass grades – A, B and C, and two Fail grades – D and E. Any result which is lower than grade E is unclassified. Certificates are issued to successful candidates and these show the overall grade. In addition, candidates receive results slips with an exam profile showing more details about their performance in individual papers.

⋆ ⋆ ⋆

Finally, let's look at the language used in CAE exam papers. Like most exams, CAE sometimes uses formal or specialised words in the instructions for questions. Look, for example, at the following instruction from a question in Paper 4:

Indicate the most appropriate response A, B, C or D

This could be 'translated' more simply as 'Choose the best answer'.

Now look at some more examples from CAE papers and see if you can match the part in italics with one of the words or phrases below.

Do You Speak CAE?

| Paper 1 | 1 Answer the questions by *referring to* the newspaper article. |
| | 2 Write the letter A, B, C or D *against* the number of each question. |

| Paper 2 | 3 The two sections *carry* equal marks. |
| | 4 Write to your friend *referring to* the points in the letter. |

Paper 3	5 Do not forget to *transfer* your answers on to your answer sheet.
	6 Choose the best phrase or sentence to fill each of the *blanks.*
	7 Some lines have one word *omitted.*
	8 The words you need do not *occur* in the formal letter.

Paper 4	9 You will hear *extracts* of five different people ...
	10 Decide which one on the list each speaker is *referring to.*
	11 You will hear the *piece* twice.

---

reading   next to   recording   talking about   copy   appear

short recordings   are worth   left out   mentioning   empty spaces

PRACTICE TEST 1
PAPER 1 READING

In this paper you will have four texts to read and about 50 questions to answer.
You are allowed 1 hour 15 minutes – an hour to answer the questions and 15 minutes to transfer your answers from the question paper to the answer sheet.

The papers generally contain three different kinds of question and these are described below. The important thing to remember is that you will need to approach each kind of question in a different way, using different reading skills. For some questions you need to read the whole text very carefully, for example. For others, you only need to find the key information as quickly as possible. If you don't approach the questions in the right way, you won't finish the paper in the time allowed.

Tip

■ In the exam, it's best to transfer your answers to the answer sheet after you finish each text, rather than waiting till the end of the exam. Otherwise you may run out of time at the end.

Multiple-Matching Questions

This is a new type of question. You are given a list of questions (**1, 2, 3**) and a list of possible answers (**A, B, C**) to choose from. For example:

Where is Dutch spoken?	1	**A** Germany
In which country is Hindi the official language?	2	**B** India
Which country has three official languages?	3	**C** Canada
Which countries have large French-speaking populations?	4	**D** Holland
	5	**E** Switzerland

The instructions for multiple-matching questions can vary slightly. You may have to give more than one answer to a question (as in **questions 4** and **5** above) or you may have to use the same answer more than once (as in **questions 3** and **4/5**)

The texts for multiple-matching questions are often quite long and they can sometimes appear a bit complicated, but remember that you don't need to read them in great detail and the questions are usually very straightforward.

Multiple- Matching Questions: General Advice

1 **Read the instructions very carefully** so you know exactly what you have to do.

2 **Glance at the text** – just to see what it's about and how it's organised.

3 **Look through the questions.** These will tell you what information to look for. If there are several sections, read and answer each one at a time.

4 **Scan the text for the information you need** – it may be in the same words as the question or it may be expressed in a slightly different way. Don't waste time on anything else.

Let's look at the **first text** in Test 1.

➜ Turn to page 26 and follow steps 1–3 above for the first set of questions (1–7). Then turn back to this page.

- What's the text about? What is the writer's purpose in writing it? to describe a journey ? to entertain? to offer advice? to advertise a service?
- What do the instructions ask you to do?
- Can you remember any of the headings?

The first task, matching the headings to the different sections, is quite a common one in the exam and it tests your ability to identify the main topics. Sometimes words from the headings appear in the text – these are the easy ones to match! Sometimes the same idea is expressed in different words. In other cases you'll have to read more carefully because the heading is a summary of the ideas.

Tip

- Where there's a different answer for each question, cross through the letters as you choose them, so it's easier to see what's left. Sometimes choosing one answer allows you to eliminate another. For example, choosing J here would eliminate E, and vice versa.

➡ Now complete the task and then go on to the second set of questions 8–16. When you've finished, you can check your answers on page 47.

Multiple-Choice Questions

This is a very common kind of exam question where you are given a question or an unfinished statement and you have to select the best answer from four choices. For example:

Dutch is spoken in   **A** Germany.   **B** Switzerland.   **C** Holland.   **D** Belgium.

Multiple-Choice Questions: General Advice

1 **Read the text quickly for general meaning** before you look at the questions. This will give you a general idea of the topic, the writer's point of view and how the text is organised.

2 **Don't worry about difficult vocabulary at this stage.** You might not need to understand it in order to answer the questions.

3 **Look through the questions** to see which parts of the text you need to read again more carefully. Try to *guess* what the right answer is at this stage – even if it's a wild guess, this will help you read more effectively later.

4 **Find those parts of the text** and then read them slowly and carefully.

5 Try to **work out the meaning of any words you don't know** by looking at the context.

➡ Turn to page 28 and follow steps 1–3 above for **questions 17** and **18**. Then turn back to this page.

- What is the text about?
- How do most people feel about the topic?
- What answers did you guess for **questions 17** and **18**?

➡ Now find the information in the text and answer **questions 17** and **18**.

Question 17 – The options:

A This may be true there's nothing in the text to say so. Stick to the facts in the text.

B The text says good speakers 'draw heavily on experience to develop new skills', another way of saying 'go on learning from talks they give'. This is the correct answer.

C The text uses the phrase 'natural ease' so you may choose this option if you are reading carelessly. But the meaning is different: good speakers only appear to be at ease because of the techniques they have learned.

D The text says the opposite: good speakers 'prepare well'.

Question 18 – The options:

A The writer does suggest going on a course but it isn't her main advice.

B This sounds a good idea but it is not mentioned in the text.

C The text says 'there is no substitute for getting out and doing it ... take every opportunity to do so'. This is the correct answer.

D Again, this sounds a good idea but it is not mentioned in the text.

Special points to remember:

Beware of options which
- use words from the text but give a different meaning.
- sound likely but where there's no evidence in the text.
- are 'all or nothing' and use words like *always, never, everywhere*, etc. They may say more than is really true.

➡ Now complete the questions for the second text. When you have finished, you will find the answers on page 47.

Paragraph Cloze

This is another new type of question. You are given a text with gaps in it and you have to choose from a list of possible 'fillers', which can be anything from a sentence to a paragraph.

It's often considered one of the hardest questions in Paper 1, perhaps because it's unfamiliar, but like any other question you can make life easier if you approach it in the right way. The important things are:

- to understand the **development of the writer's argument** or, if it's a narrative, the **sequence of events.**
- to look for **grammatical** or **logical** clues which can help you find the missing pieces of the jigsaw.

➡ Turn to the third text on page 30 and look at the headline. What could it be about? Now read the text but not the possible fillers.

- What is the text about? What is the 'message'?

Look at the beginning of the text. The writer begins by introducing the topic.
After the first gap there is an example to illustrate his point. But it must be a second example because of the words *Another candidate.* Look through the options to find a suitable first example.
The only possible answer for **question 25** is **F**.

Now look at the paragraph after **question 26**. Notice that it begins with inverted commas ("). This tells us that someone, probably an expert of some kind, is being quoted. So they must have been introduced. Look for a suitable paragraph.
A doesn't introduce Mr Grout – it assumes we know who he is. The answer is **B**.

Now notice clues for the other questions.

Question 27: the words before and after the gap refer to male candidates.

Question 28: the next section talks about a woman. Look for a paragraph which introduces the subject of women.

Question 29: Notice the inverted commas and '*he explained*' at the end. This means the speaker must have been mentioned again.

Question 30: This falls between two quotes from Mr Grout which make two contrasting points. In other words, there's a missing 'but'. Look for a logical link between the two.

 Now complete the questions on the third text. When you've finished, you can check your answers on page 47.

Before you tackle the fourth text, look back at the notes on multiple-matching questions on page 7.

PAPER 2 WRITING

This paper consists of two sections, with one task of approximately 250 words in each. In **Section A** there is no choice of topic, while in **Section B** you will have four topics to choose from. You have 2 hours to complete the paper.

The types of writing (or formats) you may be asked to produce include **formal** and **informal letters**, **reports** and **articles**, as well as shorter pieces like **notes** and **memos**. Usually the question states the format required but sometimes it is less specific. In this case, any suitable format will be acceptable. For example, if you are asked to write **instructions**, you could simply begin with an appropriate heading, or you could include the instructions in a letter or note. The same applies to an **account** or a **proposal**.

It's important to think about the special characteristics of each type of writing and the following notes list some of the main ones:

LETTERS need an appropriate **salutation** (*Dear Sir/Mr X,*) and **subscription** *(Yours sincerely,/faithfully,)* – make sure you know the rules for these. It's not usually necessary to write out the address(es) in full. Letters should have a suitable introduction and conclusion and be divided into clear **paragraphs.**

NOTES are even more informal than informal letters and there are no fixed rules about layout. The day, date or time is usually stated at the top; you can use a shortened address or omit the address completely; you can begin with *Dear ...*, with a first name, or just with an initial, depending on your relationship.

REPORTS should have a clear **heading**, an **introduction** and a **conclusion.** The information should be logically organised into separate paragraphs or sections and it's sometimes helpful to give these **subheadings** as well.

ARTICLES need a **headline** to give an idea of the subject and also to catch the reader's attention. They should **begin** and **end** in an interesting way and should be written with the particular age and interests of the readership in mind. For example, if the article is for a 'college magazine', it should appeal to teenagers.

REVIEWS (of books, films or magazines, for example,) should begin with an **introduction** or **overview** of the subject, include **detailed comments** on successful and unsuccessful features with reasons, and finish with an overall verdict, summing up your opinion.

INSTRUCTIONS must, above all, be clear. This means that you need to include all the necessary information and arrange it in the most **logical order.** The **layout** should be easy for the reader to follow. For a notice, you will also need a **heading.**

Marking

In general terms, your work will be assessed in two main areas:

Use of Language: in a good answer the English will be natural and effective. A good range of structure and vocabulary will be used and there will be very few errors.

Task Achievement: a good answer will cover all the main topics mentioned in the question and be likely to have the intended effect on the reader; it will be well-organised, with the ideas suitably linked, and will use an appropriate register.

Each section of the paper will be marked on a scale of 0–5 with a very good answer receiving 5 and a completely unintelligible or irrelevant answer receiving 0. Examiners have specific assessment guidelines for each question on the paper and use them in relation to the following global marking criteria.

- **naturalness** and **accuracy** of language;
- evidence of **range** of vocabulary and structures;
- completion of **task** without irrelevance or omissions;
- choice of **register** appropriate to the task;
- use of a variety of **cohesive devices**;
- clarity and consistency of **organisation**.

Other points

Length: The examiner won't count the number of words you've written. You'll only lose marks for a long answer if you've included irrelevant information, or for a short answer if you've left out some important points.

Spelling/Punctuation: You will lose marks for poor spelling/punctuation if it interferes with communication. American spelling is fine as long as it is used consistently.

Handwriting: If your work is difficult to read, you will also lose marks. If the examiner cannot read it at all, you'll get 0!

General Advice
- Read the **instructions** and the **written texts** very carefully. Underline or circle the important points – you'll lose marks if you don't do everything the question asks you to.
- Think about the **purpose** of the piece of writing, and what **effect** you want it to have on the reader. If you really try to **imagine** yourself in the situation, you will write a better, more convincing answer.
- Make a **plan** of the main points.
- Make sure you use the appropriate **layout** for the type of writing. Consider whether there are any special features of **language** or **style** you should use.
- Keep roughly to the **word limit** – but don't waste time counting every word!
- Leave time to **check** your work carefully afterwards. Don't lose marks because of careless mistakes!

Section A

The first thing you notice when you look at this section of the paper is how much reading there is to do. This makes Paper 2 in CAE a little different from most tests of writing because you have to deal with written information in some way before you can tackle the writing task. For example, you may have to select the important points from one or more texts, summarise the information or find the differences between two texts. In other words, Section A tests effective reading as well as writing.

The second important point is that you may be asked to produce more than one piece of writing – a letter and a brief note, for example. Make sure you do all the parts of the question – if you leave out one part, even if it's a very short part, you may lose half the possible marks or more.

Now let's look at **Section A** in Test 1.

➡ Turn to **question 1** on page 33 and read the instructions and the letter to Pat.

---

1 Completeness and **Relevance**

Which of the points below would it be important to mention in the letter of complaint? Which would be irrelevant? Why?

- ☐ It was Tony's birthday
- ☐ You discussed the choice of restaurant
- ☐ You saw an advert for the restaurant
- ☐ The restaurant was empty
- ☐ It was freezing
- ☐ The menu looked promising
- ☐ There was no lobster
- ☐ The waiter was scruffy and off-hand

- ☐ The kitchen was warm
- ☐ The steak was tough
- ☐ The peas were tinned
- ☐ Tony had a vegetarian dish
- ☐ Tony's food was lukewarm
- ☐ The bill was enormous
- ☐ There was a charge for bread
- ☐ There was a service charge of 20%.

What other information would you need to give? Feel free to invent extra details like dates and times, but don't change any of the information given.

➡ Look at the advertisement and the restaurant bill, and underline or circle any points which support your complaint and should be mentioned in the letter.

---

2 Planning

This is an essential stage – not an additional extra! It's the time when you decide how to organise what you want to say so that your message is as clear and effective as possible. You will need an **introduction** stating the reason for writing and then **separate paragraphs** giving details of the various problems. Your **conclusion** should say exactly what you expect the restaurant to do.

3 Layout/Language/Style

As this is a formal letter, remember how and where to put the date, salutation, and subscription. Divide the letter into paragraphs by indenting (beginning a short distance inside the margin). Remember suitable phrases for this sort of letter (*I am writing to complain about ... I must insist that you ....*)

■ **Special point to remember**

It's not a good idea to 'lift' phrases or whole sentences from the texts to use in your writing. They will probably sound wrong because the style or register is inappropriate and you will lose marks as a result. Try to express the same ideas in your own words.

Section B

Take time to read all the questions and decide on the question you can answer best. This may not be the one that looks easiest at first glance. Make sure you know what is required in each case: Do you understand the **situation**, can you imagine yourself in it? Do you know the necessary **vocabulary and structures**? Do you know how to **organise** and **lay out** that type of writing?

When you've decided on a question, read the instructions very carefully and underline or circle the key points. Many students lose marks in the exam because they leave out one or more important points. Remember, <u>every</u> word in the instructions counts!

> ➜ Turn to **Section B** on page 34 and read the instructions for **questions 2–5.** Look to see what type of writing is required in each case, what style or register would be appropriate and what special vocabulary or structure you might need.

Question 2

You are asked to write a detailed note (see notes on page 10). The question also mentions faxing the information but don't worry, there's no need for any special heading or layout. Start by addressing your friend/s (eg *Dear Tim/ Dear Tim and Mary*). After that, you'll only need the briefest of introductions, so don't waste time asking about the children's health or giving your latest news!

The writer asks for information about the education system in your country but this doesn't call for a long, detailed survey. The emphasis should be on giving the basic facts clearly and keeping to points which are relevant to the writer. If you happen to know something about the English educational system, you could mention any differences, but this isn't necessary to produce a good answer.

The second part of the question asks for practical suggestions. It's probably easiest to mention real schools that you know but if you have to invent schools, that's fine too.

Don't forget to add a suitable ending – perhaps encouraging the writer to contact you again if he or she needs further information or if you can help in any way.

Question 3

This requires an *article* (see notes on page 10) for an international students' magazine so think about the likely age and interests of the readers before you start – a touch of humour will probably be helpful. The question calls for some narrative (how your hobby started), some explanation (what appeals to you about your hobby), some information (where you go to add to your collection), and some description (a particular item you have or would like to have).

If your hobby is rather unusual, you will probably need to explain exactly what it involves first of all. If it's quite a common hobby, it may be more difficult to write about interestingly unless you have some special stories to tell. In either case, the important thing is to convey your interest and enthusiasm.

Don't forget to think of a suitable heading and to start and finish the article in an interesting way – imagine you very much want your article to be accepted for publication!

Question 4

The question asks for a *proposal* but doesn't specify a particular format. You could write your answer as a report (see notes on page 10), with a suitable heading (eg Suggestions for Additions to the Library), as a long memo, borrowing the headings from the memo in the question, or even as a letter . Whichever approach you adopt, the style should be quite formal.

The first part of the task really calls for a kind of *review* (see notes on page 10) but with the emphasis on the positive features. Bear in mind, too, that the items you recommend are for an educational institution so you should be able to argue that they will be useful for, or of interest to, a wide range of students. (Remember that you need to suggest two or more items.)

For the second part of the task, try to think of libraries you know and problems you have experienced – eg having to queue, not having anywhere to sit, difficulties with the cataloguing system, etc. Explain the problem(s) and suggest clear, practical solutions.

The main aim is obviously to make your proposal so convincing that the librarian cannot help but take up your suggestions.

Question 5

Here you need to write an *informal letter* (see notes on page 10) but one which is to be sent to a number of friends rather than just one. It's not usual to write *Dear Friend* in English, so leave a space after *Dear* – or put *Dear* (name of friend) – as if you were going to fill each person's name in afterwards.

A good answer will mention particular problems with the decoration (eg peeling wallpaper, flaking or discoloured paint, etc.) so if you don't have the necessary vocabulary, it's probably best to avoid this question. If you do attempt it, take a few moments to write down all the words and phrases to do with the topic that you know. It's very annoying to realise later that you forgot to include some really good specialised vocabulary!

The other important part of the question is to make your party sound so appealing that none of your friends will want to miss it!

PAPER 3 ENGLISH IN USE

Paper 3 is divided into three sections with about 70 questions in total, and you have 1 hour 30 minutes to complete it.

This part of the exam tests your knowledge of different aspects of the language system. These include **grammar**, **spelling** and **punctuation**, as you would expect, and also **register** (choosing appropriate words and expressions for formal and informal contexts), and **cohesion** and **coherence** (using language to link different parts of a text, or different ideas, together).

The three sections carry approximately equal marks but they each have a different emphasis.

Tip

- When you're working through Paper 3 in the practice tests, time yourself to see which parts take you the longest. Then when you take the exam, plan your time carefully so you allow enough time for each of the sections.

Section A

This section consists of two blank-filling (or 'cloze') exercises with 15 blanks to fill in each. The first focuses mainly on **vocabulary** and there are multiple-choice answers to choose from. The second focuses mainly on **structural points**, prepositions, articles, verb forms and so on, and there are no multiple-choice answers.

General Advice

- Read through the whole text before you think about possible answers – ask yourself what it's about and what the writer's purpose is.
- Notice the style – is it formal or fairly informal? The words you choose will have to fit in with this style.
- Make sure the answers you give fit logically *and* grammatically.

1 Let's look at the first cloze exercise in Test 1.

➡ Turn to 'Save money on the book that aims to save animals' on page 36 and read the text quickly. Don't think about the gaps yet! Ask yourself the first two questions listed under General Advice.

When you look at the possible answers, you will need to consider various points.

1 Does the word fit logically?
2 Does the word fit grammatically?
3 Is it *exactly* the right word for the context?

Take **question 7**, for example. The sentence refers to 'terrible results' – so do you expect a positive or negative word to fill the gap? Options **B** *interest*, **C** *care* and **D** *concern* are all fairly positive words and they don't fit the context. In addition, when we look at the grammar, we can eliminate **B** *interest* because it is followed by the preposition *in*, not *for* as in the text. The only answer which fits logically and grammatically is **A** *greed*.

In **questions 5** and **6**, the answers are linked. Looking at the options for question 6 first, we find two pairs of words which look similar and which are in the same general area of meaning. We are looking for an intransitive verb (one which doesn't take an object) so we can eliminate **A** *preserve* (you preserve food, for example) and **B** *conserve* (you might conserve your energy). **C** *revive* means to become active again and this doesn't fit the context. Only answer **D** *survive* is suitable.

For **question 5**, we need a verb which can be followed by an object (animals) and an infinitive without 'to'. This eliminates **A** *enable* and **C** *allow*, which are followed by a verb with 'to'. **D** *assist* is also unsuitable as it is usually followed by the preposition *in* or *with*. The correct answer is **B** *help* which can be followed by a verb with or without 'to'.

➡ Now do the rest of the task. When you've finished, you can check your answers on page 47.

---

2 Let's move on to the second cloze exercise in Test 1.

➡ Turn to 'Olympic Gold' on page 37 and read the text quickly without worrying about the gaps. Ask yourself the questions listed under General Advice again.

It's important to think about the *kind* of word which is needed in each space. Don't make an elementary mistake by putting in something which doesn't fit grammatically at all. It's usually easy to spot a missing article or a preposition but it may be harder to know when a verb or a linking word is needed. So remember to look at the whole sentence, not just the words before or after the space, and to look for any clues which may help.

When you read the first sentence of the text, you find that it is in two main parts, linked by the word in **question 16.** So this must be a linking word concerning time.

If you only look at the word after **question 17**, *place*, you might think you need an article or perhaps a preposition. In fact, when you look at the whole sentence, you find you need an *-ing* form verb (... there was something .....*ing*). The general meaning must be 'happening' but the verb has to combine with the word 'place'.

The answers are **16** *when* and **17** *taking*.

Now look at **question 21**. Here another linking word is needed – this time to connect two contrasting ideas: he was only of modest standard and he won the gold medal. The answer is *Although*.

Sometimes an important clue is slightly hidden. The clue for **question 22** is *teamed up* but it comes earlier in the sentence. You team up with a person, so this is the correct answer.

Points to remember:

- Correct spelling is essential – take care when you fill in the answer sheet.
- You'll lose marks if you write more than one word in each space.

➜ Now do the rest of the task. When you've finished, you can check your answers on page 47.

Section B

This section consists of two exercises with approximately 15 questions in each.

3 In the first exercise, you have to **recognise** and **correct errors** of various kinds which could include spelling, grammar and punctuation. This is a very useful kind of task which practises the skills you need to check your own or someone else's work. Usually an exercise concentrates on only one kind of error but occasionally you may have to correct two or more kinds of errors in the same exercise (there is an example of this in Test 5).

The instructions tell you to indicate the correct lines with a tick (√). You should expect there to be no more than about five correct lines in the text.

General Advice

- Read the instructions very carefully. What you need to do varies according to the kind of mistake you're correcting.
- Read the text quickly to get the general picture.
- Read it again much more carefully, line by line. It's easy to miss a mistake if you're thinking mainly about the meaning.
- When you've made all the corrections you can, read through the piece again to make sure it makes sense. Be careful to <u>spell</u> your answers correctly.

Let's look at this task in Test 1.

➜ Turn to 'The Big Sleep' on page 38 and read the instructions. Next read the text quickly, without worrying about any mistakes, to find out what it's about. Finally look very carefully at the first part of the text and answer **questions 31–35**.

The first example sentence (**0**) illustrates a typical type of error – the use of an article where one isn't needed. There's another error like this later in the text.

In line **31** the expression *builds out* probably looks unfamiliar to you, – this is because it doesn't exist! We say 'build' or possibly 'build up', so *out* is the unnecessary word.

In line **32**, there's an unnecessary preposition. The verb *help* is followed by an object (skin cells) and a verb with or without 'to' (to regenerate), as we saw in the first cloze exercise. The preposition *with* is unnecessary.

In line **33,** the phrase *do we need* looks right at first glance. But when we look at the whole sentence, we find there's no need for the auxiliary *do*.

You shouldn't have found any errors in line **34** because there aren't any! But don't forget to put a tick in the space. In line **35**, the phrase *in asleep* should look a bit strange. This is because *in* is a preposition and should be followed by a noun, not an adjective like *asleep*. The unnecessary word is *in*.

16

Points to remember: Correcting unnecessary words

In this type of exercise, look especially carefully at:

- **definite** and **indefinite articles**: think about the rules for using them.
- **auxiliary verbs** (be/do/have): check that they have been used correctly.
- **any expressions you haven't seen before**: they may not be correct.

➡ Now do the rest of the task. When you've finished, you can check your answers on page 47.

---

4 In the second exercise, you have to transfer information from a text in one register (eg formal) to a text in another register (eg informal) by filling gaps in the second text. This is a test of your ability to write in different styles and to recognise which words and expressions are appropriate in different contexts.

The choice of language depends on the **relationship** between the writer and reader (do they know each other well? Is it a fairly formal relationship?), on the **subject** (is it serious or not very important?), and also on the **situation** (is it necessary to be tactful, persuasive, forceful, etc? For example, the following are all ways of asking for information but they are suitable for very different contexts:

I should be grateful if you would send me details of the post you are advertising.

I really must insist that you provide a full explanation for your actions.

Could you let me know your thoughts on the matter when you get a minute?

General Advice

- Read the first text very carefully. Notice not only the information but also the **context** for the second piece of writing.
- Read the second text very carefully. Notice the style and study the example.
- Remember you can use one or two words (but no more) and you can't use words which appear in the first text.
- Make sure you give exactly the same information and that the language fits grammatically *and* stylistically.

➡ Turn to task 4 on page 39 and read the formal information. Don't worry about words you don't know for the moment. Next read the informal note and notice the style. Then look at **questions 46–51.**

- What examples of formal language can you find in the first text?
- What do you think the relationship between the writer and the reader is?
- What examples of informal language can you find in the second text?

In the example **0**, notice how the passive structure *Reservations should be made ...* becomes *We have to arrange things ...* . For **question 46**, we need an expression which means the same as *14 days*. It must be a noun because there's an article before it. The answer is *fortnight*.

For **questions 47** and **48**, we have to find another way of expressing *subject to the availability of accommodation and flights*. For **question 48**, we know we need a verb to follow *can* and that the meaning is 'obtain'. The verb must also combine with *us*, which follows. The answers are *depends (on)* and *find* or *get*.

For **questions 49–51**, we again need to express a formal sentence more simply. Instead of *We suggest that*, we must find an adjective to follow *It's ....* For *full payment*, we need a noun meaning 'quantity' to follow *whole*. For *preparation of travel documents*, we need an adjective to go with *get* (things). The answers are *advisable, amount* and *ready*.

➡ Now do the rest of this task. When you've finished, you can check your answers on page 47.

Section C

This section consists of two exercises designed to test your ability to 'recognise, produce and organise written English appropriately'. There are usually 12–15 questions in all.

5 In the first, you have to choose the best phrase or sentence to fill gaps in a text. Like the paragraph cloze exercise in Paper 1, this tests your understanding of the way the text is organised and the way the writer develops the argument. Here the missing parts are shorter – just a phrase or sentence.

➡ Turn to 'Migraine Headaches' on page 40 and read through the text.

It's important to notice that in the first paragraph the writer is talking about ordinary headaches, while migraine headaches are discussed in the rest of the text. So, for **question 60**, we need a sentence which makes this distinction and links the two paragraphs.

The second paragraph describes the main characteristics of migraine headaches compared to ordinary headaches, so **question 61** should mention one of these differences which also relates to the sentence which follows.

The answers are E and J.

Notice clues for the other questions:

62 The sentence before describes how migraine attacks vary from person to person. Is this the only variation?
63 The two sentences which follow talk about the danger of doing certain things *in excess*. Look for a sentence which mentions this idea of excess.
64 The sentence before says that not having enough food can be harmful. Is this the only thing the body needs?
65 The text has mentioned things we do which can cause migraine attacks and the sentence before advises us to stop doing them.

➡ Now do the rest of this task. When you've finished, you can check your answers on page 47.

6 In the second exercise, you have to **expand some abbreviated information** – a set of notes or an advertisement, for example – into a fuller form. You must write no more than **one sentence** for each set of notes.

The words which are usually left out of notes include **articles**, **prepositions**, **auxiliary verbs** and **linking words**, so this exercise tests your ability to produce complete, correct sentences in which the clauses are appropriately linked, where necessary. You will also need to understand some common abbreviations.

Can you explain the following?

hr./hrs.	N.B.	a.s.a.p.	Rd.
Tel.	inc.	max./min.	pop: 3000
P.S.	17th C.	St.	min./mins.
approx.	Ave.	sec./secs.	temp.

(The answers are at the end of this section.)

➡ Turn to task 6 on page 41 and read through the instruction and the notes for **questions 66** and **67**.

The example sentence **(0)** sets the style for the instructions and you should follow on in the same way. Note that there may be several ways of completing a set of notes and you would get a mark if your answer is correct, even if it is different from those suggested below or in the Key.

Question 66 needs verbs, articles, a preposition and a linking word.
Trains _go_ every _hour_ from Heuston Station (no article) *(which is) in _the_ west of _the_ city _and the_ journey _takes_ _between_ 2½ and 3 hours* (there's no need to write out numbers in full).

Question 67 needs verbs, articles, a preposition, a pronoun and linking words.
Take _a_ taxi from _the_ station _which_ _will_ _cost_ _about_ £4, _and_ tell_the_ driver _to_ _take_ _you_ to Fitton Street _which_ _is_ near _the_ Everyman Theatre.

Tips for the some of the other questions:

For **question 68,** begin with the linking word *If …*

In **question 69,** N7 and N8 refer to roads. Think of a suitable way of expressing NB here.

For **question 70,** begin with *When … ,* and think of a way of linking *2nd turning right* and *Matthew St.*

> ➜ Now do the rest of this task. When you've finished, you can check your answers on page 47.

Answers to abbreviations exercise

hour/hours; telephone; postscript (an extra piece at the end of a letter); approximately; note especially …; including; seventeenth century; Avenue; as soon as possible; maximum/ minimum; Street; second/seconds; Road; population: 3000; minute/minutes; temperature.

PAPER 4 LISTENING

The listening paper is divided into four sections with 40–50 questions in total and it takes about forty-five minutes. Here are a few general points:

The instructions for the questions are spoken on the tape as well as printed on the exam paper. The recordings in **Sections A, C** and **D** are played twice but in **Section B** the piece is played only once.

The voices you hear will speak standard English but there may be a variety of British and non-British accents. A few of the recordings used are authentic – in other words, recordings of real conversations rather than actors reading a script. This book provides practice in listening to authentic material and different accents, as do most coursebooks, so you should be well-prepared for this.

Your answers need to be correctly spelt!

At the end of the test, you have to transfer your answers on to the special answer sheet and there is time is allowed for this. Be careful, it's easy to make mistakes.

- Make sure your answers match the questions – if you overlook one answer, all the rest will be numbered wrongly.
- Don't make spelling or grammar mistakes which will lose you marks.
- Don't change your original answer by adding more details or abbreviating it.

General Advice

- **Always read the instructions carefully.** CAE uses a wider variety of question types than First Certificate and Proficiency and, unlike those exams, the details of the instructions can change from year to year.

- **Study the task.** If it's a table, look at the headings and the way it's laid out. If it's a text, read it carefully. Think about the vocabulary.

- **Look at any pictures** as they may illustrate words you don't know.

- **Study the questions** so you know exactly what information you have to listen for. If you think about the questions and try to predict the answers where possible, it will make the listening task easier.

Sections A and B

The recordings for **Sections A and B** are fairly short (about two minutes each) and are usually monologues. The questions test your understanding of specific information in the recordings and you may have to fill in missing information in a table or tick boxes, for example.

Let's look at **Section A** in Test 1. Turn to page 42 and follow these steps.

1 Read the instructions very carefully. Make sure you know exactly what you have to do.
2 Study the table. Look at the headings so you understand how the table is organised and what you need to fill in. Think about the words in the table.
3 Look at the picture. It may help you to understand some of the words in the table. Look at the illustrations for *louvre window* and *porch*, for example.
4 Study the questions. Try to predict some of the missing information. Can you suggest answers for **questions 1, 3** and **10**? Notice that the table is filled in in note form (without all the articles and prepositions) so your answers can be in note form too.

Special point to remember

- Some answers may need the **correct preposition** in order to make sense.

- Be careful with **questions 3** and **10** in this respect.

Now play the tape **twice** and answer the questions. When you've finished, you can check your answers on page 47.

Now turn to **Section B** on page 43 and follow these steps.

1 Read carefully through the instructions and the text.
2 Think about the missing information. Are there any answers you can guess?
For **question 15**, for example, what could a parent or guardian be asked to provide to say that the child did the work without any help?
3 Remember, Section B is played **once only** so it's obviously important to listen very carefully.

Special point to remember

- Sometimes the information in the recording uses slightly different words from those in the question. Be ready for this. For example, in question **14**, *Entries should be no longer than ...* is expressed as *the maximum length for each entry ...* . There is also a change of wording in **question 19.**

Now play the tape **once** and answer the questions. When you've finished, you can check your answers on page 47.

Section C

Section C is longer than the other sections (about four minutes) and is usually a dialogue or an interview. The questions test your understanding of the text as a whole, including the speaker's **attitude,** as well as specific information you hear. You may have to complete a set of notes or answer multiple-choice questions.

With note-completion, marks are awarded for the correct **key word(s)** so there is no need to write a full, grammatically complete sentence. There is only enough space on the answer sheet for about three words and if you try to write more, you'll simply be wasting time.

Turn to **Section C** in Test 1 on page 43 and follow these steps.

1 Read the instructions and the text.
2 Try to predict answers – for example **questions 20**, **21** and **27**.

Special point to remember:

■ Make sure your answer fits grammatically.

For example, in **question 27** the word *by* must be followed by an *-ing* form and you may need to make a small change to the verb form you hear. Similarly, in **questions 21** and **31**, *to* must be followed by an infinitive.

⌨ Now play the tape **twice** and answer the questions. When you've finished, you can check your answers on page 47.

Section D

Section D consists of a number of short extracts (up to about 30 seconds each) with pauses between them. You may be asked to identify things like the **context** (the situation where people are speaking), the **topic** they are talking about, or the **function** (whether they are apologising, complaining and so on).

Turn to **Section D** on page 44 and follow these steps.

1 Read the general instructions and the instructions for Task One.
2 Look at the pictures and think about the name for each item, if you know it, and also how it is used.
3 Read the instructions for Task Two and the list of reasons.
4 Be prepared for the information to be given in slightly different words from the question.

Special point to remember:

● Sometimes the precise answer isn't stated and you have to use clues in the recording to work out what the answer is. Listen carefully for the clues. In Task One, for example, the clues to **question 34** are in *bodywork*, *interior*, and *tyres*. Can you find the clues for the other questions?

⌨ Now play the tape **twice** and answer the questions. When you've finished, you can check your answers on page 47.

PAPER 5 SPEAKING

In the interview, you will be examined with another candidate and there will be two examiners. One examiner is there to work with you, explaining the tasks and helping with any problems, while the other assesses your English. The whole interview lasts about 15 minutes and there are four phases which are designed to test different speaking skills.

Most people find it less stressful to be examined with another candidate and if you are in a pair with a friend, it will probably help you to feel more relaxed. If you haven't met your partner before, however, don't worry. Working with someone you don't know can have advantages too – it may be easier to think of genuine questions to ask and more natural for you to exchange information.

Here is a summary of what happens in each of the four phases.

Phase A (About 3 minutes) In this phase the examiners will introduce themselves, and you and your partner will be expected to take part in a relaxed conversation and talk about your backgrounds, interests, career plans and so on. This phase tests your **general social English**.

Phase B (3 or 4 minutes) You will be given pictures to describe and comment on and each candidate will have a chance to talk for about a minute. This phase tests your ability to **give information clearly** and to **express** your **personal reactions**.

Phase C (3 or 4 minutes) You will have to solve a problem or reach a decision about something by discussing the matter with your partner. This type of activity is designed to test your ability to **express opinions** and **reasons** and to **negotiate a decision** with your partner.

Phase D (3 or 4 minutes) In this phase, you have to report to the examiners the decision you reached in Phase C and perhaps develop the discussion further with them. This phase tests your ability to **report, summarise** and **explain** clearly.

Marking

In the Speaking Paper marks on a scale of 0–8 are awarded by the examiners according to six separate criteria:

- **Fluency:** speaking with natural speed and rhythm, and without hesitating too much.
- **Accuracy:** using structures and vocabulary correctly or with only a few minor errors which do not obscure the message.
- **Range:** using a wide range of structures and vocabulary to communicate in a variety of contexts.
- **Pronunciation:** using English pronunciation features (sounds, stress, rhythm and intonation) accurately enough to convey the message clearly.
- **Task Achievement:** dealing effectively with the tasks. This includes contributing fully and appropriately, and showing independence, flexibility and resourcefulness in carrying out the tasks. NB It is *how* you tackle the tasks which is assessed, not whether you arrive at the "right" answer.
- **Interactive Communication:** playing an active part in the discussions and being responsive both to your partner and to the examiners.

General Advice

- Don't be afraid to ask the **examiner** to repeat something you haven't heard or to <u>clarify</u> something you haven't understood. This is much better than losing marks because you haven't done what you were asked to do!

- Remember that you are expected to co-operate with your **partner**. You will lose marks if you try to do all the talking or if you don't listen and respond to what your partner says.

- Don't be afraid to ask your **partner** to repeat or clarify something you haven't understood. You will be assessed on your individual performance and you won't lose marks if you have difficulty in understanding your partner.

Let's look at the four phases in more detail.

Phase A

In this phase, the examiners will introduce themselves to you and you will be expected to introduce yourself or maybe to introduce your partner, if you know him or her. Here is some useful language:

Responding to the examiners: *How do you do?* You reply: *How do you do?* *I'm ..../My name is ....* You reply: *I'm pleased to meet you.*	**Introducing your partner:** *May I introduce my friend/partner ....* *He/She comes from ....* *We're both studying in the same school* *We've known each other for ....* *Actually we've just met!*
Introducing yourself: *My name is .../I'm .... and I come from ....*	

As the conversation develops, you should be prepared to answer questions (or ask your partner) about such general topics as:

- your family
- the place you live
- how you travel to work/school/college
- why you're learning English
- your plans for the future
- your interests and hobbies

If you're studying in Britain, you may also be asked specific questions about the main differences compared with your own country , or about aspects of British life that you especially like or dislike.

When the examiner suggests that you ask your partner a question, try to put the question into **your own words** so that it sounds as natural and conversational as possible. Remember, too, that this is an **advanced level** examination. Try to go beyond the level of boring 'small talk' and introduce some really interesting points into the conversation! Listen carefully to your partner and show interest in what they say.

> ➡ Turn to page 45 and look at the questions in Phase A of Test 1. Think about the answers you would give and also how you could ask your partner for information as naturally as possible.

Tip
- If you're going to do the interview with someone you know, it's not a good idea to prepare together for phase A or to learn short dialogues by heart. It's always obvious to examiners if you've rehearsed beforehand and you'll get more marks for spontaneous communication.

Phase B

In this phase you will work with pictures (photographs, drawings, cartoons, etc.), and you will be asked to sit facing your partner so that you can't see each other's picture(s). You will each have a task which gives you the chance to speak for about a minute.

For each task, the idea is that one candidate does all or most of the talking. It's not meant to be a question and answer session. So, if your partner has a picture to describe, you should listen carefully and compare your own picture (the examiner will usually supply a piece of paper for you to make notes on). You will have a chance to ask brief questions at the end if necessary, but no more. When your partner has finished, you may be asked to make a few brief comments about similarities or differences in your own picture.

There are two main types of picture prompt:

Single Pictures

One candidate describes a picture. The other candidate listens in order to carry out a task. Here are some typical tasks.

Compare and Contrast – (two similar pictures) – find two or three things which are the same and two or three things which are different in the pictures.

Spot the Difference – (two pictures which are nearly the same) – find as many differences as possible between the two pictures.

Describe and Locate – (one picture showing a map, plan or layout of room and one blank plan) – mark the position of various items on the plan. If you can't draw, you can simply write the words in the right positions. Don't worry, you won't lose marks if you don't position the items correctly.

Describe and Draw – (one picture and one blank sheet of paper) listen to your partner and draw what they describe. You won't lose marks for bad drawing!

Describe and Relate (two different pictures but with a common theme) – work out what the two pictures have in common.

➡ Turn to page 45 and follow the instructions for Task 1 in Phase B of Test 1.

After you finish the task, compare your pictures carefully and discuss how you could have improved your performance. What else could you have said to describe the picture better? What vocabulary could you have used? Ask your teacher for any words or expressions you didn't know and make a careful note of them. (You may be interested to know that the pictures show the same family group photographed in 1971 and then in 1989.)

Pictures Sets

One candidate is given a set of pictures and has to describe one or more of them. Here are some typical tasks:

Each candidates has the same 8 pictures but in a different order.
Candidate A describes one or two pictures – Candidate B has to identify them.

One candidate has 6 pictures; the other has the same pictures in a different order plus a seventh.
Candidate A describes six pictures – Candidate B has to describe the extra one.

Each candidate has four pictures but one in each set is different.
Candidate A describes their four pictures – Candidate B describes the one they have which is different. The important thing with both these types of tasks is to try to do more than simply describe what you can see in the picture. If you talk about your **personal reaction** to what you see, you'll be able to use a wider range of language and you should earn more marks.

➡ Turn to page 45 and follow the instructions for Task 2 in Phase B of Test 1.

After you finish the task, study the pictures and discuss your performance again. Make a note of useful vocabulary.

Section B: Tips

■ Don't worry if you can't think of the *exact* word for something. This happens to everybody sometimes! You won't be expected to know very specialised vocabulary and you won't lose marks if you use another suitable word or find an alternative way of expressing what you want to say.

■ Try not to end negatively by saying something like 'Sorry, that's all I can think of!'.

Phase C

In this phase you will work with your partner to solve a problem or reach a decision about something. This task is intended to give you the opportunity to express your own opinions and also respond to your partner's views. In other words, it should be a discussion rather than an argument, and the emphasis should be on **co-operation** and **negotiation** rather than winning or losing! Aim for a *balance* where each person has an equal amount of time to express their views and where you really *listen* to each other. Useful language to practise would include:

asking about and expressing **opinions**	**persuading**
asking about and giving **reasons** for opinions	expressing strong **agreement**,
asking for and making **suggestions**	mild **disagreement**, etc.

You should discuss your ideas fully and try to reach agreement but if you have to agree to disagree in the end, that's all right too. You will be marked on how well you tackle the task and on the language you use, not on the results you reach.

Here are some typical tasks:

Cartoon – decide what point the cartoonist is trying to make, say whether you agree or disagree.

Photograph – work out what the photograph represents. Talk about the topic.

Set of pictures – (representing places, jobs, equipment, etc.) – choose the ones you would prefer/the ones which would most appropriate for a particular purpose; put them in order of importance.

Photograph/picture – think of a name for a new invention/discovery/development, etc.

➡ Turn to page 46 and follow the instructions for Phase C of Test 1

Tip

- When you practise for Phase C, it's a good idea to record your conversation if possible. Afterwards you can listen to the recording and see how balanced the discussion was and how wide a range of language you used. If there isn't a tape recorder available, you could ask another student to listen to your discussion and comment on these points.

Phase D

In this phase, you tell the examiners about your discussion in the previous phase and report any decisions you reached, together with your reasons. It's a good idea to practise this part of the interview too because you'll need to be able to **summarise**, using reported speech, and **explain** clearly.

Very often, you will be asked a few more questions related to the same topic. This may be because the examiners haven't quite decided on your marks, because one of you hasn't spoken very much or just because they're interested in your views! If there aren't any more questions, don't worry, it's probably because the examiners have already heard enough to make a clear assessment.

Finally, don't forget to thank the examiners and say goodbye!

PRACTICE TEST

1

PAPER 1 READING
1 HOUR 15 MINUTES

Answer **all** questions.

First text/questions 1–16

Answer questions 1–16 by referring to the newspaper article about taking children on long-distance flights on page 27.

For questions 1–7, choose the most suitable heading for the various sections of the article from the list A – J below. One heading is given on page 27 as an example.

1 Section A	**A**	Keep children under control
2 Section B	**B**	Be flexible
3 Section C	**C**	For heaven's sake, go
4 Section D	**D**	Know the safety procedures
5 Section E	**E**	Fly economy class
6 Section F	**F**	Make friends
7 Section H	**G**	Stop worrying, relax
	H	Book your seats in advance
	I	Use the flight attendant
	J	Enjoy the benefits of business class

For questions 8–16 answer by choosing the sections of the article A – H, on page 27.

Note: When more than one answer is required, you may give the answers in any order.

Which section mentions

children's clothes?	**8**	....		
a road accident?	**9**	....		
features of airline seats?	**10**	....		
airline food?	**11**	....		
sleeping arrangements?	**12**	....		
other passengers?	**13**	....	**14**	....
examples of children being difficult?	**15**	....	**16**	....

Look, daddy, I can fly

Long-haul journeys with children can be made bearable if you are well-prepared, David Thomas writes.

The following tips are the fruits of my recent experience of travelling with children who had never flown before, and the experts' advice.

A

The key to successful family flying is to ensure that you have a row of seats entirely to yourselves, so that you can spread out and scatter toys without fear of inconveniencing other passengers. Most airlines are fairly co-operative when it comes to dealing with children, but you must arrange things well in advance.

While you are reserving your seats, arrange for special meals for the children. Given any relevant information about allergies or dietary needs, most airlines will supply basic food that stands more chance of being consumed by choosy children than the normal meals served. They may also serve children before the main meal is handed out.

B

For anyone used to the comforts of Club Class, holiday offers that allow business class travel for a small extra payment may seem tempting. There are, however, two arguments against them.

The first is that while the seats in business class are incomparably more comfortable than those in economy, they tend to have fixed armrests. In economy armrests can be raised, which comes in handy.

Secondly, your fellow passengers are likely to feel far less well-disposed to disruptive young kids if they have just paid a fortune for a little comfort. In economy, the whole place is already half-way to being a cattle truck, so youthful disruption is far less noticeable.

C

No matter how well-behaved a child may be, and no matter how generously supplied with toys, no little boy or girl can sit still and silent through a transatlantic flight. As the children charge up and down the aisle, parents usually follow, apologising as they go, like neurotic cowboys, riding off to round up their runaway calves. The children become resentful, stubborn and, most crucial of all, loud. The row that ensues causes far more disturbance than the children alone could ever have done.

The moral is, let your children have a bit of a runaround. With any luck they will not do anything too drastic. But just in case they do …

D

As early as possible in the flight, introduce yourself and your children to the occupants of neighbouring rows. Assure everyone that if they feel disturbed by the children, they only have to mention it to you and action will be taken immediately. This will put you on the side of the angels and will also ensure that nobody dares to say anything.

E

The aim, remember is for the children to be as happy as possible for the duration of the flight. So be ruthless in pursuit of this aim. If your son believes that his Batman costume is the ultimate in travel-wear, do not object. You may feel embarrassed being accompanied by a tiny version of the Dark Knight of Gotham City, but he will be happy.

F

No matter how perfect your preparations, there will be moments in a long flight when danger threatens. In our case this happened when our two-year old adamantly refused to be seat-belted when required. Luckily, the attendant was able to exert her authority where ours had failed. Something about her uniform, her manner and her air of power seemed to do the trick. So, if in doubt, press the panic button and leave it to the experts.

G *Take pillows*

This is the key to everything. The four-seat row in the middle of a 747 is wide enough to allow two small children to sleep on the floor (except at take-off and landing, or when seat belts should be worn), but the floor, naturally enough, is hard. Airline pillows are insufficient to cope with the problem, but if you take an extra small pillow for each child, it should do the trick. This will allow parents to stretch out across the whole row of seats, giving them more room than they would have had in Club Class.

H

No matter how hellish your journey may be – and ours was not helped by a three-hour delay on the tarmac at Gatwick airport, followed by a taxi ride at the far end during which the driver ran over a cow – it is amazing how soon all is forgotten once you get to your destination. This is truly a case in which the end justifies the means. So if you are thinking of taking the family long distance, do not hesitate. Just go.

From *The Times*

Second text/questions 17–24

*Read the following article and then answer the questions on page **29**.*

Secrets of talking your way to the TOP

By PHILIPPA DAVIES Managing Director of London-based communication specialists VOICEWORKS

You could be one of those lucky people who seem to be naturally good at public speaking. It is unlikely that you were born with this ability. Great speakers are instinctive and inspired. They also prepare well, learn performance technique and draw heavily on experience to develop their skills.

What passes for a natural ease and rapport with an audience is often down to technique – the speaker using learned skills so well that we can't see the 'seams'.

Body language

You can learn to speak effectively in public by going on courses and reading manuals. But there is no substitute for getting out and doing it. If you dislike speaking in public, then take every opportunity to do so – even if you only start off by asking questions at the PTA meeting.

When you speak in public, almost all the aspects that make up your total image come under scrutiny. Your posture, body language, facial expression, use of voice and appearance all matter. The focus of attention is such that it can feel as though your presentation skills are under examination through a microscope.

The situation is often stressful, because the speaker is being observed and judged by others. Small quirks, like speaking too quietly or wriggling, which are not particularly noticeable in everyday communication, become intrusive and exaggerated in front of an audience.

Stereotypes

It is hardly surprising, then, that some of us feel it is easier to pretend to be somebody else when we are speaking in public. We assume a 'public speaking image' that has nothing to do with our real selves.

We sense that speaking in public is connected to acting and so we portray stereotypical roles like 'the infallible authority', 'the super-smooth sales person', 'the successful superwoman'. Unfortunately, if we don't really feel like these types, then we will look as though we are striving for effect.

For instance, you could decide that you want to play the life and soul of the party when you speak, although, in actuality, you are a rather quiet person who rarely uses humour. You read that humour works well in public speaking so you decide to tell a few jokes.

You look ill at ease when you do so and your timing leaves a lot to be desired. Your talk misfires badly. You will not have been true to yourself and your audience will have been reluctant to trust you. You need to find your own style.

The most skilled actors use their own feelings and experiences to help them inhabit character. As a public speaker, you have more scope than most actors – you have your own script, direction and interpretation to follow. You can even rearrange the set and choose the costume if you like.

The most successful speakers are obviously projecting an image but one that rings true. They project the best aspects of themselves – 'edited highlight'. The serious quiet person will project serenity and consideration for others. The outrageous extrovert will use humour and shock tactics. Speaking in public is a performance and one in which you present a heightened version of your personality.

To speak well, there needs to be a balance of impact between speaker, message and audience. If one of these elements overpowers the other two, say if the speaker is over-concerned to project personality, or the message is rammed home without due regard for the type of audience, or the speaker allows him or herself to be thrown by a noisy crowd – then the performance will suffer.

Your image helps maintain this balance. If you get up to speak dressed like a Christmas tree, then your appearance will be overpowering. Delivering your message in an over-stressed and, therefore, over-significant tone of voice, will encourage your audience to switch off. When you start to speak, if your body language and facial expression remind the audience of a frightened rabbit, then you won't gain its confidence.

The audience

Both in planning and in presentation, the speaker's main consideration should be the audience. When we are in an audience, we make two important decisions about speakers. Do they have credibility (Do we trust them? Have they authority? Do we respect them?) and can we identify with them (Do they understand our problems? Have they shared experiences in common? Do we have any similar values?).

The biggest block to effective public speaking is attitude. If you think you can't and you never will be able to, you won't. Speaking in public is something anyone can learn to do. Be positive and accept setbacks as part of the learning process. A much quoted statistic from the Book of Lists, shows that the majority of people fear public speaking more than death!

17 The author says that the best public speakers

    A   are professional actors.

    B   go on learning from the talks they give.

    C   feel naturally at ease with people.

    D   don't need to plan their talks in advance.

18 Her main advice to beginners is to

    A   attend a course on public speaking.

    B   ask good speakers for advice.

    C   get as much practice as possible.

    D   study other speakers' performances.

19 Some speakers pretend to be someone else because

    A   they feel less self-conscious.

    B   they don't want to be recognised.

    C   they've been advised to.

    D   they enjoy acting.

20 This approach is not recommended because

    A   it will make the audience laugh.

    B   it is likely to look false.

    C   it can make the talk last too long..

    D   the audience will complain.

21 The best speakers

    A   use visual aids

    B   tell stories and jokes

    C   learn the scripts of their talks by heart.

    D   present their most positive characteristics.

22 The author warns against

    A   being too emphatic in what you say.

    B   getting into arguments with the audience.

    C   making the audience feel nervous.

    D   wearing coloured clothing.

23 One thing the audience will judge a speaker by is whether he or she

    A   gets the balance of the talk right.

    B   has prepared the talk properly.

    C   is someone they can relate to.

    D   is someone with power.

24 Overall, the author's message is that public speaking is

    A   something few people can do.

    B   the most frightening thing you can do.

    C   a talent some people have naturally.

    D   a skill that can be developed.

*For questions **25–30**, you must choose which of the paragraphs **A – G** match the numbered gaps in the extract from a newspaper article. There is one extra paragraph which does not belong to any of the gaps.*

Job seekers ill-suited for interviews

BY RODNEY HOBSON

JOB Hunters are abandoning the suit and dressing in outrageous clothes in order to stand out from the other candidates.

25

Another candidate, determined to show the prospective employer how desperately he needed the job had large holes in his shoes.

26

'Examples of odd interview attire offered by managers taking part in a survey we conducted varied from the merely inappropriate to the provocative, and even revolting: earrings, pony tails, shorts, bright yellow suits and pink cord-uroys were listed. And that was just for men.'

27

In a slightly different approach, another man tried to unsettle the interviewer by refusing to take off his overcoat although it was a sweltering hot day and the interview room was warm.

28

One woman showed how much she felt at home in the office by finishing off her interview attire with a rather delightful pair of gold slippers. Laddered tights, loud and revolting ties, sunglasses and tattoos were cited as pet hates on the interview circuit.

29

'In creative environments such as advertising, people can get away with more unconventional dress than within, say, accountancy,' he explained.

30

'You are likely to score more points in that crucial time by looking smart and professional rather than by trying to stand out from the crowd with a style of dress that may be alien and ridiculous to the interviewer.'

A

Mr Grout said: 'To increase your chances of getting a job at the interview stage, you need to play the interview game and ensure that you are appropriately dressed for the profession and the position.

B

Jeff Grout, Managing Director of Robert Hall, the financial recruitment specialist, said: 'Many interview candidates are abandoning the conservative suit and sensible shoes for a look that is bound to get them noticed – but for the wrong reasons.

C

While the men tended to be unconventional or just plain scruffy, the women dressed to kill.

D

Another female candidate, who was extremely thin, managed to turn up in a suit which she had apparently borrowed from a friend several sizes larger.

E

'However, as the decision to hire is made within the first five minutes of the meeting, possibly before the candidate has spoken, dress and personal presentation are the key to the decision-making process.

F

One young hopeful sped into the interview room on a skateboard.

G

Other male candidates made their mark at important interviews by turning up in a boiler suit, baseball boots or different colour socks.

From *The Times*

Fourth text/questions 31–50

*Answer questions 31–50 by referring to the newspaper article on page 32. Choose your answers from the areas **A – F**, which are mentioned in the article.*

*Note: When a question requires more than one answer, you may give the answers **in any order**. Some choices may be required more than once.*

Remember to read the questions before you read the text in detail so you don't waste time on parts which aren't important.

A Australia	**D** Maldives	
B Cozumel, Mexico	**E** Philippines	
C Hawaii	**F** Thailand	

In which areas have the coral reefs been damaged by the following causes?

industry	31		
dynamite fishing	32	33	
Crown of Thorns starfish	34	35	
spear fishing	36		
coral collecting or mining	37	38	39 ....
pollution from resorts	40		

Which areas offer the following attractions?

unique fish	41	
good visibility	42	43 ....
good value diving	44	
snorkelling tours	45	46 ....
shark feeds	47	
the fish with the longest name	48	

Which areas have the following problems?

There is overcrowding in some places	49 ....
It's expensive to get to the coral reefs	50 ....

Questions 44 and 50: Look out for places where the information is expressed slightly differently in the text.

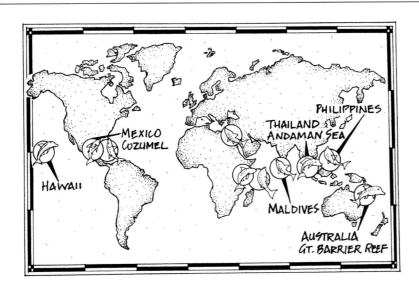

In search of the fish with the longest name

MARINE PARKS

Marine tourism – and conservation of coral reefs – is booming all over the tropics. NICK HANNA reports

AUSTRALIA

The 100,000-mile Great Barrier Reef is the largest and most complex reef system on the planet. Its 2,900 individual reefs are divided up into a complex set of zones comprising the world's biggest marine park, home to more than 1,500 species of fish and 400 species of coral.

Since the reef is 30 to 45 miles offshore, most people visit on a day trip: these operate from resort islands as well as from Cairns, Port Douglas and Townsville. The cost of these trips can be prohibitive, and in this respect the Barrier Reef isn't as satisfying as somewhere, say, such as the Maldives, where you can just stumble out of your room and take a short swim to the reef at the edge of the lagoon.

A recent innovation in marine tourism here has been the introduction of guided snorkelling tours with marine biologists, which give you a 'hands-on' experience of the reef and an opportunity to touch corals and other marine life safely.

Like reefs all over the world, the Great Barrier is not without its share of ecological problems, the most notable of which, as we wrote two weeks ago, is the destruction caused by population outbreaks of Crown of Thorns starfish, which literally eat the reef.

COZUMEL, MEXICO

Cozumel, a small island off Mexico's Yucatan peninsula, is another success story for marine parks. Although the island's reefs were popular with divers as long ago as the 1960s, the reef environment deteriorated badly in the 1970s through uncontrolled spear-fishing (which took care of the larger fish) and the harvesting of coral for the souvenir trade. However, thanks to the foresight of the Mexican government in declaring the reefs a marine refuge in 1980, fish populations are now thriving and divers are flocking there.

Cozumel is divided from the mainland by a deep-water channel which is swept by rich currents, ensuring not only flourishing marine flora and fauna, but also guaranteed good visibility (normally in excess of 100ft). The underwater terrain is unique in the Caribbean, with colossal coral buttresses riddled with caverns and tunnels.

Cozumel is to American divers what Egypt and the Red Sea are to their European counterparts: good-value, good-quality tropical diving: currently the best bargain in the Caribbean.

HAWAII

Thanks to its relatively recent volcanic origins, the Hawaiian archipelago is markedly different underwater from other tropical locations. Reefs are limited in extent and the chief feature of the underwater geology is rolling lava formations and caves. However, these islands are the most isolated tropical islands in the world, which means that a high proportion of marine species are endemic. Many of these biologically unique fish are very beautiful indeed, and snorkelling or diving here is a distinctive experience, a rewarding combination of stark, primal topography and brilliantly-coloured fish.

On the main island of Oahu, 12 miles to the east of Waikiki Beach, Hanuama Bay is one of the most successful marine parks in Hawaii. Once a favourite fishing ground for Hawaiian royalty, the reefs were severely depleted until the area became a marine life conservation district in 1967. Since then, recovery has been remarkable, and there is now an abundance of beautiful tropical reef fish, including hordes of tangs and jacks, surgeonfish, butterflyfish, wrasse and parrotfish, as well as the fish with the longest name in the world, the Humuhumunukunukuapuaa (Hawaii's state emblem). The one drawback of Hanuama bay is that the water is almost as crowded with people as it is with fish; go early in the morning.

MALDIVES

Although there are no official marine parks or protected areas, the diving and snorkelling is generally superb. There are well-equipped dive centres on most tourist islands and snorkellers will find that in very few other countries is the magic of the underwater world as guaranteed as it is here. Large, tame fish abound on nearly every reef and in some lagoons you'll find yourself completely surrounded by what seems like a circular wall of fish, as if you were floating in a gigantic tropical aquarium.

Some reefs do have problems most noticeably because of coral being mined for building, and pollution from resorts, but overall they appear to be in good shape.

Shark feeds are common in the Maldives, and many divers enjoy the opportunity to observe the power and grace of these magnificent creatures underwater.

PHILIPPINES

These are more than 13,000 square miles of reefs in the Philippines but thanks to dynamite fishing, coral souvenirs and hurricanes, a considerable proportion are dead.

Although there are as yet no national marine parks, there are protected areas where you can find good diving and snorkelling. Some of the best reefs are around Palawan; at the diving resort of El Nido on the northwest corner of the island, they've made a concerted effort to protect their reefs, as well as setting up feeding stations, which are frequented by large groupers, jacks, needlefish and barracuda.

There is a cluster of dive resorts in the Balangas area near Anilao, two hours south of Manila. Boats go out to Sombrero Island, a popular dive spot with surprisingly intact coral cover. This is one of the better dives I had in the Philippines: sadly, the exception rather than the rule.

THAILAND

The most extensive reefs in Thailand are in the Andaman Sea, on the west coast. This includes the area around Phuket, although many reefs in the immediate vicinity of Phuket have been smothered and killed by dredging for tin, which was the principal industry here before tourism.

Some of the best diving is in the Ko Similan National park, 50 miles north of Phuket, and there are regular departures for three- to five-day trips to these islands. Although there is some damage from dynamite fishing and Crown of Thorns starfish here, fish life is abundant enough to satisfy most people and visibility can reach 125ft-plus during the season. The best developed reefs are beyond the Similans in the Ko Surin National Park, near the Thai/Burmese border.

Reefs around Koh Samui and Koh Phangan on the east coast have been damaged by dynamite fishing and bottom trawling. Snorkelling trips operate from Koh Samui to the nearby Ang Thong National Park, but this suffers from similar problems and I found it disappointing.

From *The Sunday Times*.

Instructions to candidates

*This paper contains one Section A task and four Section B tasks. You must complete the Section A task and **one** task from Section B.*

The two sections carry equal marks.

*Read the instructions and consider the information **carefully** both for section A and the task you select for Section B.*

Section A

1   After seeing an advert for a local restaurant, you and your friend Tony went there last Friday but it was an expensive and disappointing evening. You've described the experience in a letter to a friend.

Read the restaurant advertisement, restaurant bill and the extract from the letter and then, **using the information carefully**, write the letter described in the instructions on page 34.

THE
Golden Fork
RESTAURANT

**Cuisine for the appreciative diner
Reasonable prices**

Open Tuesday to Friday

Specialities:

- seafood
- steaks
- game
- vegetarian dishes
- Indian curries
- desserts

With its cosy atmosphere and friendly staff, The Golden Fork would like to welcome you and your family for an unforgettable evening. All our food is freshly prepared and we use only the finest ingredients.

Telephone: 463271

THE
Golden Fork
RESTAURANT

Telephone: 463271

Table Number: 1	Date: 14/11

Steak	£15.99
Vegetarian hot pot	£12.99
Chocolate mouse	£3.50
Cheesecake	£2.50
House red	£10.00
Coffee	£2.50
Bread	£1.00
	48.48
Service 20%	9.70
TOTAL	£58.18

Dear Pat,

You asked how Tony's birthday celebration went. Well, after a lot of discussion and consulting various restaurant guides, we saw an advert for a place called the Golden Fork which looked interesting and had had good reviews. All I can say is it's not a good idea to believe everything you read!

When we arrived we were the only ones there - hardly a good sign! The place was absolutely freezing – maybe they didn't think it was worth wasting money on heating for just the two of us – but anyway we had to keep our coats on through-out. The menu looked quite promising, actually, but they were completely out of lobster which was our first choice. The waiter was pretty scruffy and off-hand and we got the distinct impression he was more interested in getting back to the kitchen where it was warmer! In the end, I had a steak which was as tough as old boots, with peas which were obviously tinned. Tony had some vegetarian dish which they'd obviously heated up in the microwave but not for long enough because it was lukewarm.

The bill was the last straw! It was enormous – they'd charged extra for bread (which we didn't eat), and included a service charge of 20%, would you believe it? In the end we just paid the bill and went, we were too miserable to make a fuss. Thinking about it later, though, and looking at what it says in their advert, we've decided to write and complain in the strongest terms. If they don't give us our money back, we're going to write to each and every one of those restaurant guides and put them in the picture!

Write a suitable **letter of complaint** to the Golden Fork Restaurant.

You must lay out the letter in the appropriate way but it is not necessary to include addresses.

Section B

Choose ONE of the following writing tasks. Your answer should follow exactly the instructions given. Write approximately 250 words.

2   An English family you know are coming to spend a year living in your country and they will be staying quite close to you. This is part of a letter which you receive from them.

We're all very excited about our 'year out' but one thing which we need to sort out is the children's education. I'm afraid I know very little about the system in your country - do you think you could give me some general information – eg the different levels, when the school year begins, how long the school day is, whether you have to pay for books, etc? John is five, as you know, and Alice will be ten by the time we arrive. Could you also suggest some schools in the area which I could contact to see if they've got places? If you could fax this information straightaway we'd be really grateful

Write **a detailed note**, covering all the points raised in the letter, which can be faxed to your friends.

3 An international students' magazine is running a series of articles on the things people collect, usual or unusual. Write **an article** about something you collect, describing how your hobby started, what you find interesting or satisfying about it, and where you go to find additions to your collection. Mention any item which you are particularly pleased to have and/or that you would particularly like to have.

4 You have received this memo from the librarian at your school/college.

Memo	
From:	B. Snary (Librarian)
To:	All Staff and Students

As you know, a proportion of our budget each year is set aside for purchasing new additions to the library. These can be books, videos, or subscriptions to magazines and newspapers, and they can be in any language.

We would welcome your suggestions as to how this money should be spent. Please put your ideas in writing, explaining clearly how the items you recommend would be of benefit to the institution as a whole. Any other ideas as to how the library service could be improved would also be welcome.

Write **a proposal** mentioning two or more additions that you would like the library to have and one way in which the library service could be improved.

5 You've just moved into a new flat. It could be very nice but the decoration is in a terrible state at the moment. You can't afford to have it redecorated professionally so you'd like to get your friends to help you and you think a 'painting party' might be a good idea. Write **a letter** which you can copy to a number of friends telling them about the flat and your idea for a party. Try and persuade them that it would be fun to come along and lend a hand.

Answer **all** questions.

Section A

1   For questions **1–15,** read the advertisement below and then decide which word best fits each
     space. The exercise begins with an example (**0**).

Save money on the book that aims to save animals

Do you want to (**0**) ....take..... part in the battle to save the world's wildlife? *Animal Watch*
is a book which will (**1**) .... you in the fight for survival that (**2**) .... many
of our endangered animals and show how they struggle on the (**3**) .... of extinction.
As you enjoy the book's 250 pages and over 150 colour photographs, you will have the
(**4**) .... of knowing that part of your purchase money is being used to
(**5**) .... animals (**6**) .... From the comfort of your armchair, you will be
able to observe the world's animals close-up and explore their habitats. You will also discover
the terrible results of human (**7**) .... for land, flesh and skins.

   Animal Watch is packed with fascinating facts. Did you know that polar bears cover their
black noses (**8**) .... their (**9**) .... so they can hunt their prey in the snow
without being seen, for example? Or that (**10**) .... each orang-utan which is captured,
one has to die?

   This superb (**11**) .... has so (**12**) .... Britain's leading wildlife
charity that it has been chosen as Book of the Year, a (**13**) .... awarded to books
which are considered to have made a major contribution to wildlife conservation. You will find
Animal Watch at a special low (**14**) .... price at all good bookshops, but hurry while
(**15**) .... last.

0	**A** play	**B** be	**C** take	**D** have
1	**A** combine	**B** involve	**C** bring	**D** lead
2	**A** meets	**B** opposes	**C** forces	**D** faces
3	**A** edge	**B** start	**C** limit	**D** end
4	**A** satisfaction	**B** enjoyment	**C** virtue	**D** value
5	**A** enable	**B** help	**C** allow	**D** assist
6	**A** preserve	**B** conserve	**C** revive	**D** survive
7	**A** greed	**B** interest	**C** care	**D** concern
8	**A** with	**B** by	**C** for	**D** from
9	**A** feet	**B** claws	**C** paws	**D** toes
10	**A** with	**B** by	**C** for	**D** from
11	**A** publicity	**B** periodical	**C** publication	**D** reference
12	**A** imposed	**B** impressed	**C** persuaded	**D** admired
13	**A** symbol	**B** title	**C** trademark	**D** nickname
14	**A** beginning	**B** preparatory	**C** original	**D** introductory
15	**A** stores	**B** stocks	**C** goods	**D** funds

2 *For questions* **16–30**, *complete the following article by writing the missing words in the spaces provided.* **Use only one word in each space.** *The exercise begins with an example* (**0**).

OLYMPIC GOLD

In April 1896, an Irishman (**0**) ......*by*...... the name of John Pius Boland was in Athens

visiting the famous German archaeologist, Schliemann, (**16**) .... it came to his ears that

there was a sporting event (**17**) .... place in the city.   Being a keen tennis player, he

decided to investigate further and discovered (**18**) .... his surprise that the event in

question was none other (**19**) .... the first ever Modern Olympic Games and that

(**20**)............... a variety of events it included a tennis tournament. (**21**) .... only of modest

standard, he borrowed a pair of white flannel trousers and a racquet, entered and won the gold

medal. Encouraged by his success, he teamed up in the Men's Doubles (**22**) .... a

German, Fritz Krauern, and won that too – thereby earning himself a place in the record books

(**23**) .... the first man to share an Olympic gold medal with (**24**) .... of another

nationality.

'The important thing in the Olympic Games is not winning (**25**) .... taking part,'

declared the founder of the Modern Olympics, the Baron de Coubertin. Doubtless

(**26**) .... who fought well and won in those first Games felt every bit (**27**) ....

satisfied with their achievements as any of today's medal-hungry competitors when the time

came to line (**28**) .... in front of a table and step forward to receive their rewards. (The

victory podium incidentally, along (**29**) .... flags and national anthems, was not intro-

duced (**30**) .... the Los Angeles Games of 1932.)

From High Life

Section B

3 In **most** lines of the following text, there is **one** unnecessary word. It is either grammatically incorrect or does not fit in with the sense of the text. For each numbered line **31–45**, find the unnecessary word and then write the word in the space provided. Some lines are correct. Indicate these lines with a tick (√). The exercise begins with two examples (**0**).

THE BIG SLEEP

Since the time immemorial we have put our trust in a good night's   **0**   _the_

sleep to help us look and feel better. And with good reason: sleep   **0**   ✓

restores the body, builds out muscle, strengthens bones and the   **31**   _____

immune system and helps with skin cells to regenerate. But just   **32**   _____

how much sleep do we really need is a matter of debate. Back in   **33**   _____

the 9th century King Alfred the Great was the first to decide that a   **34**   _____

third of the day - eight hours - should be spent in asleep. Though   **35**   _____

we still use Alfred's idea as a yardstick, but we all find the sleep   **36**   _____

patterns which suit us best. While it's true that too much or too   **37**   _____

little of sleep can cause headaches, drowsiness, lack of energy   **38**   _____

and irritability, it's the *quality* of sleep or rather than the quantity, **39**   _____

which are matters. Since man's earliest days, all sorts of medicines   **40**   _____

and drugs have been tried to achieve deep, untroubled sleep.   **41**   _____

However, to get away from artificial methods, the exercising during   **42**   _____

the day and avoiding such indigestible food, caffeine-filled drinks   **43**   _____

and alcohol just before bedtime can help you to sleep better. And   **44**   _____

the right kind environment is very important. You need to be in   **45**   _____

darkness, warm – but not too warm – and comfortable.

WHAT DO <u>YOU</u> DO IN BED?

According to a recent survey:

21 per cent of people in Britain take job-related paperwork to bed.

44 per cent watch TV in bed

34 per cent have a phone in the bedroom

52 per cent of bedrooms have a stereo

59 per cent of people like to drink in bed

34 per cent like to eat in bed

61 per cent read magazines in bed

24 per cent keep exercise bikes in the bedroom

4 *For questions **46–59**, read the following information from a holiday brochure and use the information to complete the numbered gaps in the informal note. **Use no more than two words** for each gap. The exercise begins with an example (**0**). The words you need **do not occur** in the brochure information.*

Formal information

1. Reservations
Reservations should be made through your travel agent, at least 14 days in advance. Late bookings, up to three days in advance, can be accepted but are subject to availability of accommodation and flights. We suggest that late bookings be accompanied by full payment to expedite preparation of travel documents.

2. Visas
Tour participants shall ensure that they comply with all visa and health requirements of countries they intend to visit. If in doubt, tour participants are advised to consult their travel agent.

3. Amendments
Tour itineraries may be extended in duration and extra sightseeing tours may be added. Please ask your travel agent for extra night rates and Optional Tour prices.
All modifications and extensions must be made at the time of booking. Changes made after travel documents have been issued are subject to an amendment fee of US $50. No changes can be made after departure.

4. Cancellations
For all tours, a fee equivalent to 10% of the tour price will be payable if confirmed bookings are cancelled within five days of departure.

Informal note

Jane - *Re: the holiday.*

I've been looking through the brochure again and I think we'd better act fast. We have to

(0) ....*arrange*.... things through a travel agent, so I'll call in to 'Worldwide Tours' tomorrow. As it's

less than a (46) .... before the departure date, it all (47) .... whether they can

(48) .... us hotels and flights for the dates we want. Let's keep our fingers crossed they can!

Apparently, at this late stage it's (49) .... to pay the whole (50) .... rather than

just the deposit, so there's time for them to get the tickets and things (51) .... The

brochure says it's (52) .... us to make sure we have all the (53) .... visas and

injections. That's something I'll (54) .... with the travel agent. There's a note in the small

print to say we can make the trip a day or two (55) .... or (56) .... some extra

sightseeing tours if we want. We'd have to decide now, though, because they (57) ....

an extra fee to change the tickets later and you can't make any changes once the trip

(58) .... By the way, I hope you're not thinking of changing your mind because we

(59) .... get all our money back if we cancelled!

Lyn

Section C

5   *For questions **60–65**, read through the following text and then choose from the list **A – J** the best phrase or sentence given below to fill each of the blanks. Write one letter (**A – J**) in each space. **Some of the suggested answers do not fit at all.** One answer has been given as an example (**0**).*

Migraine Headaches

Nearly everyone has had a headache at some time or another - and if it is only an occasional thing you won't need to seek help from your doctor. The most common type of headache, which affects 80 per cent of people at some stage of their lives, is the tension headache. (**0**) *.H.*

(**60**) ..... It is now known that during an attack measurable changes take place in chemicals in the body which are not seen in other types of headache.

(**61**) ..... In between attacks you feel completely well. The headaches usually last up to three days and often affect only one side of the head. You feel sick and you can't stand bright lights. A small number of people experience flashing lights before their eyes. And when the attack is over many people feel totally washed out.

Although there are five identifiable stages of a migraine attack, not everyone experiences all of them, and no two people will have attacks of the same duration, frequency and severity. (**62**) ..... They can become more frequent and more severe for no apparent reason, or stop for several months or even years.

Migraine seems to be caused by an inherited susceptibility, combined with a response to certain internal and external factors. (**63**) ..... The triggers of a migraine attack are many and varied, but most of them, in excess, can harm the body. For example, lack of food: the body needs fuel and cannot go too long without it. (**64**) .....

Although there is no absolute cure for migraine, it can be controlled. Discovering your own triggers and dealing with them can help you have fewer attacks, and put you in control. (**65**) .....

From *The Sunday Express Magazine*

A   Even within each person, attacks change with time.

B   The same applies to lack of sleep.

C   An attack is your body's way of letting you know that you are pushing things a little too far.

D   Or the pain can be quite vague and may be present most of the day with little change.

E   Migraine, however, is something different.

F   Remember, bad habits can be overcome.

G   Others have times when they get as many as two attacks a week.

H   Hunger, sleeping in or being overtired are other factors which can cause headaches.

I   It is very rare to have an attack over the age of 40.

J   Unlike tension headaches, migraine attacks do not occur daily.

6 *Use the following notes you've made about how to reach a friend's house to prepare a set of instructions for someone else to follow. Write **one complete sentence** for each numbered set of notes, using connecting words and phrases, as appropriate. You may add words and change the form of the words given in the notes but do not add any extra information. The first point has been expanded for you as an example (**0**).*

---

0 Train or car Dublin to Cork but train probably easiest.

66 Train: every hr from Heuston Station (in west of city) – journey 2½–3 hrs.

67 Taxi from station (£4?) – tell driver Fitton St near Everyman Theatre.

68 Car: Journey 4 hrs (at least!) depending speed/any stops.

69 N7 to Portlaoise – N8 to Cork – follow signs city centre (NB complicated one way-system!)

70 Find South Mall – 2nd turning right (Matthew St)

71 Fitton St – 1st left (before Everyman Theatre)

72 Jan's house on left – red door, lion's head doorknocker.

73 Any problems ring Jan (021 – 583001).

---

0 You can travel by train or car from Dublin to Cork but the train is probably the easiest way.

66

67

68

69

70

71

72

73

Section A

You will hear some information about home security. For questions 1–11, complete the table by filling in the missing information.

You will hear the recording twice.

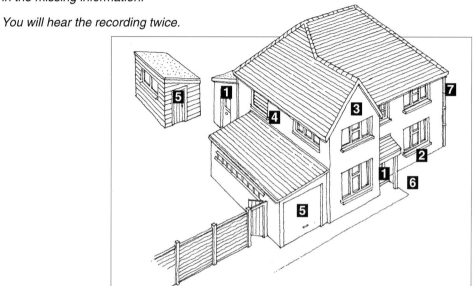

Area	Problems		Solutions	
1. Front, back & side doors	Inadequate locks can be		Fit strong locks	
	1			
2. Downstairs windows	Provide easy		Fit strong locks	
	2			
3. Upstairs windows	Can be reached from roof or		Fit strong locks	
	3			
4. Louvre windows	Glass panels		Fit lock or replace with	
	4		**5**	
5. Garage or garden shed	Can provide useful		Use a good padlock or	
	6		**7**	
6. Unlit porch	Callers cannot be		Fit a	
	8		**9**	
7. Drain pipe	Provides a means			
	10		**11**	
	upstairs windows		close to drain pipe	

Section B

You will hear about a competition for young writers. As you listen, you must fill in the information for questions 12–19.

*Listen very carefully as you will hear this piece only **ONCE**.*

Bookworm Young Writers' Competition

Rules

1. Open to children aged **12** [____] on the closing date.

2. Any **13** [____] of writing (poetry, prose or drama) will be accepted.

3. Entries should not be longer than **14** [____] words.

4. Each entry must be accompanied by a **15** [____]
   from the entrant's parent or teacher, certifying that the work was composed unaided.

5. All sheets must be numbered and **16** [____].

6. Entries must be sent to the following address:

   Young Writers' Competition

   17 [____]

   TAUNTON
   Somerset TA1 5QT

7. No entries will **18** [____].

8. The **closing date** is **19** [____].

Section C

You will hear an interview with Robert Miles, who works as a Flight Service Director for an airline. For questions 20–31 complete the sentences with an appropriate word or short phrase.

You will hear the piece twice.

What Robert enjoys about his job is the chance to travel and to **20** [____] different people.

What he doesn't enjoy about his job are the **21** [____].

In his previous career, he worked in the **22** [____].

He originally intended to stay with the airline for **23** [____].

He gets between **24** [____] days off during a working period.

43

Working for Cabin Crew Management allows him to find out what goes on

| 25 | | in other departments.

His most famous passenger has been | 26 | | .

He helps nervous passengers by | 27 | | them, and also by taking

them on to the | 28 | | so they can see what goes on.

The passengers who make his life difficult are those who make | 29 | | .

When he started in his job, it was possible to offer a more | 30 | |
service to passengers.

The other change is that nowadays he has to | 31 | | sectors.

Section D

You will hear five people talking about bargains they have bought.
You will hear the recording twice.

Task One

For questions 32–36, look at the eight pictures labelled A–H. As you listen, put the pictures in order by completing the boxes 32–36 with the appropriate letter.

SPEAKER 1	32
SPEAKER 2	33
SPEAKER 3	34
SPEAKER 4	35
SPEAKER 5	36

Task Two

Letters A–H list possible reasons for people selling things cheaply to the different speakers. Decide which one on the list fits the situation in each case. For questions 37–41, put the letter of the description against the appropriate speaker.

SPEAKER 1	37
SPEAKER 2	38
SPEAKER 3	39
SPEAKER 4	40
SPEAKER 5	41

Which speaker bought something cheaply because the owner

A   wanted to sell it quickly?

B   couldn't afford to keep it?

C   didn't have enough room for it?

D   didn't like it?

E   knew it was faulty?

F   didn't realise it was valuable?

G   didn't know how to use it?

H   had never used it?

P A P E R   5   S P E A K I N G
APPROXIMATELY 15 MINUTES

Work with another student.

Phase A

(about 3 minutes)

Imagine you had never met your partner.

- Introduce yourselves to each other.

- Tell your partner a little bit about yourself. Listen to what your partner says and ask one or two questions.

- Find out why your partner is learning English. Explain your own reasons.

- Tell your partner about a special interest or hobby of yours. Find out what interests your partner has.

Phase B

(3 or 4 minutes)

Task 1 (Compare and Contrast)

In this part of the test you will each have a picture to look at. The pictures are similar but not the same. Don't look at each other's pictures.

Candidate A: Turn to the picture on page 137 and describe what you can see.
You have about a minute.

Candidate B: Turn to the picture on page 138 and listen to your partner's description. You can make notes on a piece of paper if you wish. When A has finished, mention **two** things which are the same as, and **two** things which are different from A's picture. Do you think the pictures could be related in some way?

Now compare pictures.

Task 2 (Describe and identify)

You will each have the same set of pictures showing fashions from the past but they are arranged in a different order. Don't look at each other's pictures.

Candidate B: Turn to the set of pictures on page 138 and describe the clothes worn by **two** of the women, so that your partner can identify them.

Candidate A: Turn to the set of pictures on page 137. Listen to your partner's description and decide which two pictures are being described. If you still need help at the end, you can ask your partner one or two questions. What helped you to identify the pictures?

Phase C

(3 or 4 minutes)

Look at the cartoon below. Talk about it and decide what the cartoonist is saying.
Do you agree with the cartoonist's point of view? Why/ Why not?

Phase D

(3 or 4 minutes)

In this phase the examiner would ask you to report your conclusions about the cartoon and then ask a few more questions about your views on the influence of television in modern society.

To practise your reporting skills, work with another pair and take it in turns to summarise and explain the conclusions you reached.

Details of marking scheme for this paper can be found on page 22.

Paper 1

First Text
Look, daddy, I can fly

1 H	6 I	11 A
2 E	7 C	12 G
3 G	8 E	13/14 B, D
4 F	9 H	15/16 C, F
5 B	10 B	

Second Text
Secrets of talking your way to the top

17 B	20 B	23 C
18 C	21 D	24 D
19 A	22 A	

Third Text
Job seekers ill-suited for interviews

25 F	27 G	29 A
26 B	28 C	30 E

Fourth Text
In search of the fish with the longest name

31 F	42/43 B, F
32/33 E, F	44 B
34/35 A, F	45/46 A, F
36 B	47 D
37/38/39 B, D, E	48 C
40 D	49 C
41 C	50 A

Paper 2

See notes on marking and assessment criteria on page 11.

Paper 3

Section A
1 Save money on the book …

0 C (example)		
1 B	6 D	11 C
2 D	7 A	12 B
3 A	8 A	13 B
4 A	9 C	14 D
5 B	10 C	15 B

2 Olympic Gold

0	by (example)
16	when
17	taking
18	to
19	than
20	among(st)
21	(Al)though
22	with
23	as
24	someone
25	but
26	those/someone/anyone
27	as
28	up
29	with
30	until

Section B
3 The Big Sleep

0	the (example)	38	of
0	√ (example)	39	or
31	out	40	are
32	with	41	√
33	do	42	the
34	√	43	such
35	in	44	√
36	but	45	kind
37	√		

4 Re: the holiday

0	arrange (example)
46	fortnight
47	depends (on)
48	find /get
49	advisable/sensible/best
50	amount
51	ready/to us
52	up to
53	necessary
54	check (on)
55	longer
56	do/take/go on/add (on)
57	charge
58	has begun/started
59	wouldn't/couldn't

Section C
5 Migraine headaches

0 H (example)		63 C
60 E		64 B
61 J		65 F
62 A		

6 Dublin to Cork

Answers should be marked according to a 0–1–2 scale:

2 Acceptable response linking the ideas successfully, with only minor errors.

1 Response successfully communicates the information required, but with major error(s).

0 Response communicates the wrong information and/or errors seriously impede intelligibility.

The following are example answers. Other versions are possible and marks should be awarded as appropriate.

0 *(example)*
66 Trains go every hour from Heuston Station in the west of the city and the journey takes between $2\frac{1}{2}$ and 3 hours.
67 Take a taxi from the station, which will cost about £4, and tell the driver to take you to Fitton Street, which is near the Everyman Theatre.
68 If you're travelling by car, the journey will take at least 4 hours depending on the speed you drive at and whether you make any stops.
69 Take the N7 to Portlaoise and then the N8 to Cork where you should follow the signs to the city centre but be careful because there's a complicated one-way system.
70 When you have found South Mall, take the second turning right, which is Matthew Street.
71 Fitton Street is the first turning on the left before you get to the Everyman Theatre.
72 Jan's house is on the left and it's got a red door with a lion's head doorknocker.
73 If you have any problems, you can Jan ring on 021 583001.

Paper 4

Section A
Home Security

1	easily opened
2	access
3	with a ladder
4	slide out
5	ordinary windows
6	burglary tools
7	remove tools
8	identified
9	security light
10	of reaching
11	Secure windows

Section B
Writing Competition

12	16 or under
13	original piece
14	3,500
15	signed statement
16	pinned together
17	P.O. Box 2,000
18	be returned
19	September 12th

Section C
Flight Service Director

20	look after
21	long hours
22	public service
23	two years
24	18–28
25	behind the scenes
26	the Queen
27	reassuring
28	flight deck
29	unreasonable demands
30	personalised/personal
31	fly longer

Section D
A Real Snip

32 F	36 D	39 A
33 E	37 D	40 F
34 H	38 H	41 C
35 G		

PRACTICE TEST

2

PAPER 1 READING
1 HOUR 15 MINUTES

Answer **all** questions.

First text/questions 1–24

Answer the following questions by referring to the extract from a leaflet published by a wildlife organisation on page **49**.
Choose your answers from the animals **A–G** which are listed below.

Animals

A Addax
B Scimitar horned oryx
C African elephant
D Mountain gorilla
E Walia ibex
F Northern white rhinoceros
G Cheetah

For questions **1–11**, answer by choosing the animals which are in danger for particular reasons.
Indicate the answer to each question by choosing from the list of animals **A–G**.

Note: When more than one answer is required, you may give the answers **in any order**. Some choices may be required more than once.

<table>
<tr><td>

You will often find the actual words of the question in the text, but for **questions 5–10**, you need to look for different ways of expressing the same idea.

</td><td>

Which animals are in danger for the following reasons?

They have lost their habitat.   1 ....   2 ....   3 ....   4 ....

They are deliberately killed.   5 ....   6 ....   7 ....   8 ....

                                            9 ....   10 ....

They are accidentally killed in military operations.   11 ....

</td></tr>
</table>

*These questions ask you about the numbers of particular animals. Indicate your answers by choosing from the list **A–G** on page **48**.*

Which animals are the following statements true of?	
Numbers have actually increased in recent years.	**12** ....
There are probably less than 100 left.	**13** ....
Nobody knows how many there are left.	**14** ....
There are still relatively large numbers.	**15** ....
Numbers could be halved in the next ten years.	**16** ....
There are probably less than 500 (but more than 100) left.	**17** ....

To locate the information quickly, look for topic words like numbers, population, estimate and also actual numbers – but be careful! – some of the numbers refer to other aspects of the problem.

*These questions ask you about the animals mentioned in the text. Indicate your answers by choosing from the list **A–G**.*

*Note: When more than one answer is required, you may give the answers **in any order**. Some answers may be required more than once.*

Which animals are mentioned as being hunted for part of their body?	**18**	**19** ....
Which animal is mentioned as surviving in desert areas?	**20**	
Which animals are mentioned as living on open grassland?	**21**	**22** ....
Which animal is capable of living in several different habitats?	**23**	
Which animal does not need a supply of running water to survive?	**24**	

Every day, somewhere in the world, another species becomes EXTINCT
In this part of Africa alone, all these creatures are in danger

Addax

Addax nasomaculatus

Close to extinction. Formerly throughout entire Sahara. Decline due to uncontrolled killing and loss of habitat due to competition for scrub grass with domestic animals of nomadic tribesmen. No accurate estimate of current numbers. Remnant population in desert areas far from water, lives most of its life without ever drinking, deriving sufficient moisture from the plants it eats.

Cheetah

Acinonyx jubatus

Numbers now reduced to an estimated 15,000, evenly distributed throughout sub-Saharan Africa. At present rate of loss the numbers could decline by half in the next ten years. Cause of decline is loss of habitat and poaching of skins. Inhabitants open grassland and savanna scrubland. Requires fairly long grass in order to approach within 100 metres attacking distance of prey.

Scimitar horned oryx

Oryx dammah

Endangered. Extinct north of Sahara. Now only found in very small numbers between Mauritania and the Red Sea Sahel. Decline due to hunting and loss of habitat.

Walia ibex

Capra walie

In severe danger of extinction. Possibly only 300 left in most impregnable parts of Simien mountains in Ethiopia but some estimates put population as low as 150–200. Grazes on grassy terraced uplands. Major cause of decline is loss if habitat by erosion of land due to poor agricultural practice.

African elephant

Loxodonia africana

Though still numerous compared to the rhino species, the elephant is in severe danger because of the sale of poaching for its tusks. Estimates put this at up to 100,000 a year killed, which could decimate populations in many parts of Africa in less than 10 years. Only recently, Belgian customs officials uncovered the largest single shipment of ivory ever seized outside Africa – a container of 2000 elephant tusks.

Widely distributed throughout Africa, south of the Sahara. Well adapted to deserts scrub, thorn bush, uplands and sub-tropical forest.

Mountain gorilla

Gorilla gorilla beringei

Poachers have reduced the mountain gorillas of central Africa to a dangerously low number. Five years ago in Rwanda the number was estimated at only 250 – though it has increased since then as a result of conservation work supported by WWF. Now we are working in the impenetrable forest of Uganda and Zaire to save the small population of surviving gorillas.

Northern white rhinoceros

Ceratotherium simum cottoni

Highly endangered. In 1984 there were 500 remaining in the wild. Now the number is probably less than 50, distributed thinly in Zaire. Poaching and military operations have so drastically reduced its numbers that it is in severe danger.

Inhabits grassland and the verges of acacia woodland. Grazes entirely on grass.

The black rhinoceros (Diceros bicornis) is also extremely vulnerable. Numbers now down from 65,000 in 1970 to less than 4,000 at the last survey.

There is still time to save these animals if we act NOW

Second text/questions 25–30

Read the following article and then answer the questions on page 51.

Is the office fit for the job?

SAFETY

Help is now at hand for the terminally challenged. **Paul Bray** reports on the latest legislation

As the number of people who work with computers has risen, so worries about possible harmful effects have grown. Now the risks of eye strain from the glare of screens and muscular injuries from constant tapping at keyboards are to be recognised by a new law.

From January 1, a European directive, called Work with Display Screen Equipment, will be implemented in Britain to attack lazy employers who fail to create a healthy and safe working environment. It will deal with eyesight risks, physical problems and mental stress, and obliges employers to assess their employees' computers, furniture, offices and working practices.

Too few employers have prepared for this change, however. The government's Health and Safety Executive has hardly any resources for publicising the new law, and its principal ergonomist,* Dr Colin Mackay, admits that "there are bound to be organisations that haven't a clue that this is going to happen,"

Understandably, the bulk of the publicity has been generated by manufacturers with ergonomic furniture or low radiation screens to sell. This has focused attention on the equipment, at the expense of issues such as working practices and software design.

Of course, having the right equipment is essential. But if used badly–too intensively, badly adjusted, badly serviced, in the wrong light and so on – even the best equipment will not prevent problems such as muscle and tendon injuries, backache, headaches and mental stress.

The equivalent would be having a car tuned and serviced, then driving it non-stop for eight hours a day, with a dirty windscreen and your knees jammed against the steering wheel.

Many problems stem from ignorance and lack of forethought. "The general problem is that computers have just been dumped on people's desks," says Trevor Shaw, an ergonomist employed by Cleveland county council. "Neither users nor managers have given much consideration to what changes should be made to their working environment."

Focusing on equipment has scared many employers into thinking they will have to shell out vast sums on new hardware. For many, however, simple measures such as turning screens away from windows to avoid glare, teaching users how to adjust chairs, or re-allocating work so nobody spends too much time at a computer, may be enough.

Rest breaks from the computer need not mean coffee breaks. Staff can do other work, such as manning the phone, opening the post or filling the photocopier. Overall, employers should see the new law not as an imposition, but as an opportunity to abandon the "production line" mentality of computerised offices in favour of a more comfortable, more productive way of working.

Mackey says: "If you say 'what's the minimum I've got to do to comply', it will probably backfire and you'll have all kinds of industrial relations problems. If you do it properly, it'll help you operate more efficiently."

All new equipment installed after January 1, must comply with the regulations. The onus for inspection and implementation is on employers. Users must be given training in health and safety matters and the use of the system. Jobs must allow periodic breaks and changes of activity to reduce time spent at the screen. There are also rules on equipment, such as separate keyboards, flicker-free screens, adjustable chairs, adequate desks, footrests, document holders, and even window blinds. Equipment already in use before January 1 need not comply until 1996; but it must be assessed straight away.

Anyone with doubts about computer health and safety should consult a doctor or other expert.

ergonomist: someone who studies how working conditions, machines and equipment can be arranged so that people can work more efficiently

From *The Sunday Times*

25 Dr Colin Mackay is concerned that some employers

  A don't know about the new law.
  B don't care about the new law.
  C are very worried about the new law.
  D won't be able to obey the new law.

26 Most of the publicity about the new law so far has concentrated on

  A office design.
  B office equipment.
  C new working practices.
  D new computer software.

27 According to the article, problems can arise when office equipment is not

  A replaced frequently.
  B switched off frequently.
  C used in the right conditions.
  D connected correctly.

28 The writer explains that many problems could be solved by

  A spending a large amount of money.
  B giving staff more coffee breaks.
  C sending staff on training courses.
  D making small changes to working practices.

29 Dr Mackay believes that obeying the new law fully will lead to

  A fewer mental breakdowns.
  B more industrial relations problems.
  C lower costs.
  D greater efficiency.

30 From January 1st, all existing equipment must

  A meet the new regulations.
  B be adapted to meet the new regulations.
  C be checked to see if it meets the new regulations.
  D be replaced with equipment which meets the new regulations.

Questions 27 and 28:
Sometimes the correct answer summarises information in the text.

Questions 29 and 30:
Sometimes the correct answer expresses information from the text using different words.

Third text/questions 31–36

*For questions **31–36**, you must choose which of the paragraphs **A–G** on pages **52** and **53** match the numbered gaps in the newspaper article. There is one extra paragraph which does not belong in any of the gaps.*

BACK-CHAT

If your heart skips a beat when you realise you are about to talk to an answering machine you most definitely aren't alone.

31

Top psychologist Dr David Lewis has examined what lies behind the problem that appears to be peculiar to us Britons, and now offers some solutions. Our American cousins certainly have no trouble talking to machines (14 per cent of Americans have answering machines against two or three per cent in the UK).

▶ **32**

So, are past problems in dealing with answering machines putting off these potential owners - despite the fact that they realise the enormous benefits?

▶ **33**

• Technophobia is experienced by people who have an inherent fear of machines of all types. Technophobes can easily be identified by conversations which develop in this way: "Hello, oh no, don't tell me I'm talking to a machine ... oh ... oh ... call me back."

To help techno-fear sufferers Dr Lewis recommends planning messages carefully whenever you need to make a call. If you are caught unawares ring off, write down the key points - then redial. You must be sure to give your name, phone number, the date and the time as well as a brief message.

• Some people have problems with answering machines because they need constant feedback during a conversation even if only with grunts of understanding and/or approval.

34

• Other people encounter difficulties with machines because they need time to warm up to a conversation. This applies to tough calls as well as casual chats. The machine inhibits them because they feel unable to ramble on.

35

• The element of time pressure can cause problems for some. Worrying that the machine won't allow enough time for you to say all you need can cause anxiousness and, in turn, key points of the message are forgotten. In this instance Dr Lewis suggests imagining the person you want to talk to is at the other end of the phone. He also recommends writing down what you intend to say until you become used to answering machines.

• The realisation that mistakes you make will be recorded on tape can make people nervous. Dr Lewis recommends giving yourself positive feedback after leaving a message.

36

A

Yet even though there's only a small number of actual owners, a third of those questioned admitted they would find it useful to have a machine at home.

B

Denied this feedback, they tend to lose the thread of their conversations. To overcome this problem, Dr Lewis suggests practising into a tape recorder - especially if you come across answering machines at work.

C

Analyse how you did and, where there was a problem, work out a better solution for next time. If you own a machine yourself, listen to how respondents on your machine leave their messages and copy the best styles.

D

Again, by planning calls, trouble can be avoided. The message should be kept short and simple and always include an action which you want taken such as "call me back".

E

There are now many products on the market, and each new product incorporates more advanced technology. Several of the newest machines, for instance, include a remote turn-on facility that allows you to switch them on with a simple call from anywhere in the world.

Side notes:

There are two clues to help you. One is in the section before: *two or three per cent* – is this a lot of people? The other is in the following section: *these potential owners* – which potential owners?

Notice the five black dots in the text. What do they introduce? The missing paragraph will give you the answer.

Question 34: The clue here is in the section before: *they need constant feedback ...*

F

Recent research reveals that in the so-called age of technology, a staggering 45 per cent of people felt ill at ease talking to answering machines. And a further 30 per cent of those questioned actually admitted rehearsing what they wanted to say before calling.

G

Dr Lewis has looked at the phenomenon in some depth. He has identified five main fears which make talking to answering machines difficult and has come up with helpful tips on how to conquer each.

From *This is Bristol and Bath*

Fourth text/questions 37–50

Read the following letter written to a quality newspaper.

Under-developed?

From Mrs Peggy Harbidge

Sir, I have "inherited" from a young keen-green photographer friend who is moving to Bristol, a large quantity of those small plastic canisters that films come in. He had been hoping to recycle them, but it seems the manufacturers do not want to know.

Can any of your readers suggest a suitable use for these objects?

Yours faithfully,
PEGGY HARBIDGE,
The Gift Shop,
St Margarets, Dover, Kent

Read any introduction quickly – it will probably help to set the scene and get you thinking about the topic. Here the word *canister*, which you may not know, is explained.

Answer questions 37–50 by referring to the letters, on page 54, which were sent a few days later, in response to Mrs Harbidge's question.

For questions 37–50 answer by choosing from the letters A–K, on page 54.
Note: When more than one answer is required, you may give the answers in any order.

Which letter is from

the manufacturers of the film canisters?   **37** ....

someone who obtains the canisters from

other people?   **38** ....

someone who is critical of the manufacturers?   **39** ....

Which letter mentions using the canisters

for carrying money?   **40** ....   **41** ....   **42** ....

for storing sewing equipment?   **43** ....

for storing writing equipment?   **44** ....

as part of a party costume?   **45** ....

during trips abroad?   **46** ....   **47** ....

for an outdoor hobby?   **48** ....

in modern art?   **49** ....

for carrying medicine?   **50** ....

Remember that the information in the text may be expressed slightly differently.

53

Under-developed but over-used

A *From Mrs Rosemary Bailey*

Sir, I read Mrs Peggy Harbidge's letter (March 18) with great excitement. Not being a keen photographer I visit local chemists and camera shops to beg for these empty film canisters for which she seeks a use.

I am a *Brownie Guider and have endless uses for them – storing sequins, tiny beads and other small craft items. Brownies do not waste so much glue if they are given a film container with a small amount in. But our best use is for sewing kits.

Yours faithfully,
ROSEMARY BAILEY,
7 Tait House, Greet Street, SE1

B *From Mrs Melissa Hawes*

Sir, The best use is as holders of my children's pocket money. One or two can hold savings, one can hold book money and one can hold money for sweets. They can be customised by each child, labelled and even decorated. They fit neatly into pockets, are hard to drop unwittingly and the close-fitting lids are particularly important as one of my daughters has an uncanny knack of losing one pound coins.

Yours faithfully,
MELLISSA G HAWES
21 Allard Crescent,

C *From Mr D.W. Wilcox*

Sir, We have written separately to Mrs Harbidge about the recycling of plastic film containers, but would like to reassure your readers that Kodak Limited takes its "green" responsibilities very seriously.

When films are sent for processing, they should be returned in the canister. Procedures are in place for the canister in turn to be sent to recycling agents.

Yours faithfully,
D.W. WILCOX (Manager,
Corporate Public Relations
and Communications Division),
Kodak Limited, PO Box 66,
Hemel Hempstead, Hertfordshire.

D *From Ms Peni Walker*

Sir, Peggy Harbidge identifies a problem which is all too common in this country – packaging manufacturers just "don't want to know" when it comes to recycling their products. A European directive on packaging is being negotiated in Brussels – Friends of the Earth is pressing the government to agree to one which makes manufacturers responsible for ensuring that their packaging gets recycled.

In the meantime, such items could be returned to the manufactures – they created the problem, let them solve it.

Yours sincerely,
PENI WALKER,
(Recycling campaigner),
Friends of the Earth,
26–28 Underwood Street, N1.

E *From Mr J.P. Chambers*

Sir, Film canisters, complete with colour-coded lids, are ideal for separating, storing and transporting coinage from different countries. In my experience only the 50p and Swiss 5-franc piece are too big.

Yours sincerely,
J. P. CHAMBERS,
24 Green Lane, Tadworth, Surrey.

F *From Dr R. M. Pearson*

Sir, They make very suitable containers for change for parking meters.

Yours faithfully
RICHARD PEARSON
10 Clock Tower Mews,
Arlington Avenue, Islington, N1.

G *From Mr Peter Butler*

Sir, Those pesky, plastic, pots are ideal companions on overseas trips. Waterproof, light and taking little room, they have carried my pills and potions, salt, pepper and even Marmite these many years.

Yours faithfully,
PETER BUTLER,
9 Holborn, Westgate House, EC1.

H *From Mr C. J. E. Moysen*

Sir, I have found them an ideal alternative to hanging corks from your "Australian-look" outback headgear. Excellent for a fancy dress party.

Your servant,
C. J. E. MOYSEN,
3 Gaydon Road,
Bishop's Itchington, Warwickshire.

I *From Mr Julian Smith*

Sir, I find they prove invaluable receptacles for safely keeping tube flies and hooks while salmon fishing.

Yours faithfully,
JULIAN SMITH,
Egremont House, Belmont,
Nr Bolton, Lancashire.

J *From Mrs David Pentreath*

Sir, they are extremely useful for storing difference sizes of calligraphy pen nibs, and also for carrying a small amount of water for washing nibs at one's calligraphy classes.

Yours faithfully,
JUDITH PENTREATH,
The Old House,
Holt Green,
Wimborne, Dorset.

K *From Dr S. Charles Lewsen*

Sir, Mrs Harbridge would be well advised to give them to any modern sculptor, whence they are quite likely to end up at the Tate.

Yours faithfully,
S. CHARLES LEWSEN
35 Marlborough Place, NW8.

From *The Times*

* A Brownie is a junior member of the Girl Guides. Brownies are usually between seven and ten years old.

Instructions to candidates

This paper contains one Section A task and four Section B tasks. You must complete the Section A task and **one** *task from Section B.*

The two sections carry equal marks.

Read the task instructions and consider the information **carefully** *both for Section A and the task you select for Section B.*

Section A

1   You are living in an English-speaking country and have, unfortunately, had a number of items stolen from your home. Read the newspaper article which reported the burglary, the advertisement and the information on how to make a claim from your insurance company and then, **using the information carefully**, write the notice, note and statement listed on page **56**.

> Remember to read the instructions and texts very carefully, underlining or circling the key points.

> Avoid using words or phrases from the texts if possible. Try to express the same ideas in your own words.

NEWS in brief

Burglar Strikes

- A mountain bike, worth £500, a camera, a black leather jacket and £60 in cash were stolen in a burglary at a house in High Street, Membury yesterday while the occupant was absent.

  The thief forced a door to get into the house, ignoring the burglar alarm which sounded as he entered.

  The bike should be easily identifiable as the frame is painted bright pink.

Car Targeted

- Thieves stripped a Ford Escort of £3,000 worth of accessories at Redwood Motors in

DOREX
the mountain bike specialists

ALPINE – climbs tall mountains, flies over bumps. Strong enough to conquer the great outdoors yet light enough to carry. Packs quickly and easily into your car boot with quick release front and rear wheels. Minimum maintenance. Lightweight aluminium construction. 21 speeds, 20" frame. Adjustable seat.

Safe as Houses Insurance Ltd

What to do if your property is lost or stolen

1. Inform *Safe as Houses Insurance Ltd* as soon as possible.
2. Inform the police if theft is suspected.
3. Take all reasonable steps to recover the missing property.
4. Check that the loss or damage is covered by your policy.
5. Complete the claim form obtainable from the *Safe as Houses* head office.

What is covered?

Clothes and **articles** of a strictly personal nature likely to be worn, used or carried, and also **portable radios, portable TVs, sports equipment and bicycles.**

What is not covered?

Valuables (eg jewellery, watches, and coin collections) or **money** (eg coins and bank notes, postal and money orders).

Head Office: 22 Hill Street, Bridlington, BX5 4WW

Now write

(a) **a note** to *Safe as Houses Insurance* reporting the burglary and requesting a claim form (write about 50 words).

(b) **a notice** advertising a reward for the stolen mountain bike (write about 25 words).

(c) **a statement** for the police describing the circumstances of the burglary, and giving details of the stolen property and any other relevant information.

Section B

Choose ONE of the following writing tasks. Your answer should follow exactly the instructions given. Write approximately 250 words.

2   You are going to spend 6 months working abroad and you have decided that it would be a good idea to let your house/flat while you're away. You have just seen the following advertisement in a local newspaper.

> ### CITY RETREATS
>
> Don't leave your home empty while you're away. Let it work for you!
>   We have clients seeking short-term accommodation for holidays or working visits to your area.
>   If you have a house or flat you would like to let on a monthly basis, please send a full description to:
>
> Celia Swindon, City Retreats, Exeter.

Write **a report** giving all the relevant information about your house/flat, including its location, size, layout, equipment and any special features. Give details of public transport and any shopping or leisure facilities nearby.

> Your report will need a **main heading** and also **subheadings** for each section (see notes on page 10). Take time to make a plan and also a list of topic vocabulary.

3   You have recently returned from a holiday during which you experienced several problems with the travel arrangements. Since your return you have telephoned the tour company and this is part of the letter you have received.

> We are sorry that you were disappointed with some aspects of the travel arrangements for your recent holiday with "One World Travel" and regret that the service provided on this occasion does not appear to have met the normal high standards which the company is known for. In order for us to investigate your complaint fully and assess what compensation payment is appropriate, we should be grateful if you would put full details of the problems you experienced in writing.

> Notice that the company seems willing to pay you compensation so your letter should be polite but also firm. Include all the important facts and invent any extra details.

Write **a letter** describing exactly what problems occurred. You must lay this out in an appropriate way but it is not necessary to include addresses.

> You could write the review as a **report** or in the form of a **detailed note**, if you prefer. (See notes on page 10).

4   An American friend of yours who speaks your language quite well has written to ask for your advice on which newspapers from your country it would be useful to read for information and language practice. Write a **review** of the main newspapers in your country, describing their different characteristics, and recommend one or two which your friend might find interesting and readable.

5   You have been asked to write **an article** about the lives of young people for an international magazine. Describe some of the ways in which young people in your town spend their leisure time and suggest improvements in the facilities that are available which you would like to see in the future.

> Make sure you answer both parts of the question.

Answer **all** questions.

Section A

1   *For questions* **1–15,** *read the article below and circle the letter next to the word which best fits each space. The exercise begins with an example* **(0).**

Expressions with either **make** or **do** are often tested in the English in Use paper. It's a good idea to make a point of learning as many of these expressions as you can.

Oscar's Winning Performance

Two boats, engines paralysed, are drifting **(0)** ....helplessly.... towards rocks in a raging sea. Gale-force winds are blowing as a distress message is relayed to the **(1)** .... The west coast search-and-rescue helicopter takes off from Shannon; its **(2)** .... is Clew Bay in County Mayo.

The terrified crews on *Sundancer* and *Heather Berry* are only half-a-mile from disaster when Hotel Oscar, the Irish Marine Emergency Service helicopter arrives and the winch* crew **(3)** .... saving their lives. There's no **(4)** .... for the boats – the conditions are too bad for that. The threatening rocks will make matchwood of them.

It's not easy to get the rescue line down on the pitching, rolling decks as the pilot, Captain Al Lockey hovers directly **(5)** .... By the time the exhausted winchman has **(6)** .... the two crew members of *Heather Berry*, the helicopter is running **(7)** .... on fuel. The pair on Sundancer will have to be abandoned if **(8)** .... else is to survive. As if that decision isn't difficult enough, screaming winds make for a treacherous flight out of the bay.

For Captain Lockey, 25 years a helicopter pilot and veteran of typhoon conditions off oil rigs in the South China Sea, this was the worst experience in a distinguished **(9)** .... In fact, a change in wind direction was to **(10)** .... *Sundancer* its horrible fate, much to the **(11)** .... of the rescue crew whose hearts were breaking as they were forced to turn their backs and **(12)** .... for home. Medals, it is said, should be given to those who have to **(13)** .... that most painful decision to say 'no'. Fortunately, most crews can and **(14)** .... say 'yes' in all conditions and at all **(15)** .... of night and day. That was Mission 47, accomplished just over three months after Hotel Oscar's contract began in July 1991.

From *Cara* magazine.

* *winch* : a machine which is used to lift heavy objects or people who need to be rescued.

0	**A** pointlessly	**B** carelessly	**C** aimlessly	**Ⓓ** helplessly
1	**A** shore	**B** land	**C** beach	**D** seaside
2	**A** direction	**B** destination	**C** journey	**D** arrival
3	**A** set off	**B** set up	**C** set out	**D** set about
4	**A** luck	**B** way	**C** hope	**D** point
5	**A** above	**B** higher	**C** ahead	**D** over
6	**A** picked out	**B** picked up	**C** taken over	**D** taken off
7	**A** low	**B** down	**C** short	**D** out
8	**A** no one	**B** everyone	**C** someone	**D** all
9	**A** job	**B** role	**C** profession	**D** career
10	**A** spare	**B** save	**C** rescue	**D** prevent
11	**A** satisfaction	**B** comfort	**C** relief	**D** gratitude
12	**A** go	**B** fly	**C** head	**D** lead
13	**A** give	**B** do	**C** say	**D** make
14	**A** should	**B** do	**C** may	**D** need
15	**A** periods	**B** moments	**C** hours	**D** minutes

> **Question 10:**
> Three of these verbs would be followed by an object (*Sundancer*) + **preposition** + noun/-ing. Only the one that doesn't need a preposition will fit here.

2 For questions **16–30**, complete the following article by writing the missing words in the spaces provided. **Use only one word for each space.** The exercise begins with an example (**0**).

Cause for Alarm?

A friend was kept awake one night recently (**0**) ......*by*...... a car alarm. At 6 am he stormed out and tried to force the car window open. A neighbour caught him (**16**) .... the act and (**17**) ....of calling the police, brought out a hammer to help. (**18**) .... them, they broke the window, turned off the alarm, and happily went back to bed.

The owner, (**19**) .... to his car, presumably thought his expensive vehicle alarm had prevented a break-in. Precisely the opposite was true.

(**20**) .... my friend been the type who steals car radios, the alarm would have provided the perfect cover: "Stupid burglar alarms," he could have said to passers-by as he attacked the car with a screwdriver, and (**21**) .... would have taken any notice. So (**22**) .... is the point of alarms when everyone (**23**) .... from my sleepy friend, that is, ignores them?

The police, and even the manufacturers, admit (**24**) .... much. Inspector Keith Brayne of the Metropolitan Police Crime Prevention Service says: "People are ignoring them because they go off (**25**) .... the time." Keith Cobham, director of Cobra Security Systems, admits: "If an alarm goes off nobody (**26**) .... take any notice, even if the thief is disconnecting the batteries. The main deterrent value (**27**) .... you are the owner is that the thief does not know where *you* are."

But what is the likelihood of an owner remaining within earshot of his car? Most alarms automatically cut out the engine, (**28**) .... the main purpose of the noise is to deter thefts of stereos and briefcases. But as Inspector Brayne points out: "This sort of theft takes place (**29**) .... split seconds. If the person has smashed the window, he'll carry on regardless (**30**) .... the alarm."

From The Independent on Sunday.

> **Question 26:**
> Make sure you use the right **tense**. This sentence begins with *If* + present simple; what structure is that? What tense is needed here?

> This is an example of a **dependent preposition**. When you learn new nouns, verbs and adjectives, make a point of learning the prepositions which go with them.

3 In **most** lines of the following text, there is **one** incorrectly spelt word. For each of the numbered lines **31–46**, find the incorrectly spelt word and then write the correct spelling in the spaces provided. Some lines and no spelling mistakes. Indicate these with a tick (√). The exercise begins with two examples (**0**).

Remember to read the text for **meaning** before you check the **language**. It's very easy to miss small spelling mistakes when you're thinking about the meaning.

H O M E W O R K

More and more people are working from home these days. It	0	✓
reduces expences and overheads to a minimum. Less time is	0	*expenses*
waisted on travel and there is no extra rent. Accountants need	31	_____
little more than a desk, a calculator, some specialy ruled	32	_____
accountancy paper and a few refference books. Others, like	33	_____
freelance journalists, cannot manage without at least one electronic	34	_____
or electric typewriter, fax facilities and a couple of phones, plus an	35	_____
answering machine. Some find they cannot keep up with the	36	_____
workload without a home computor. It only needs a little imagination	37	_____
to convert a room into a workplace and etablish instant electronic	38	_____
links with clientes or a head office hundreds of miles away.	39	_____
Streamlining has become an art form as manufacturers, realising	40	_____
the need to compactness, have produced space-saving equipment.	41	_____
Secretaries may not be redundant but men and woman working	42	_____
from home quickly realise than machines can be as eficient, if not	43	_____
so pleasant. Home filling systems no longer need to be a bulky,	44	_____
four-drawer cabinet. An intire world of information can be stored –	45	_____
and retrieved – in a matter of moments from a single disk hardy	46	_____
the size of a saucer.		

Be careful! A word may look perfectly correct but still be spelt wrongly in the **context**.

4 For questions **47–59**, read the following informal note about a magazine competition and use the information to complete the numbered gaps in the formal announcement. **Use no more than two words** for each gap. The exercise begins with an example (**0**). The words you need **do not occur** in the informal note.

Dear Carl,

I've had an idea for December's magazine. How about having a photography competition? We could get a few people who are well-known in the field to decide on the best shots. I'm sure Mary Thorpe, editor of "You and Your Camera" would agree to help, for example, – she's a friend of my mother's. As 1st prize, we could offer that review copy of the new camera manual we were sent and I'm sure we could come up with some useful equipment (say twenty pound's worth?) for the 2nd prize. We could put the results (and also a selection of the best pictures?) in next month's magazine.

If you like the idea, you'll have to think of a topic and say when entries have to be in by. Why not print an official entry form so people have to buy the magazine? Say photos should be no smaller than 10 x 14 (cm) and that they have to send an SAE of the right size if they want their photos back, otherwise we'll have to pay the postage. One other thing – I'd add a note to say they can't blame us (or claim compensation) if anything happens to their photographs.

Mandy

Photography Competition

Enter our exciting competition by sending in your best holiday photograph and you could be a

lucky (**0**) ....*winner*......... ! Entries will be (**47**) .... by a panel of (**48**) ....,

including Mary Thorpe, editor of "You and Your Camera". The best photographs will

(**49**) .... in next month's magazine.

> **First Prize:** "Complete Guide to Photography" by Martin Webber
> **Second Prize:** Camera equipment to the (**50**) .... of £20
> **Third Prize:** Camera cleaning kit

RULES

1) The (**51**) .... for entries is 31st December.

2) Photographs can be in colour or black and white and must be of a
   (**52**) .... size: 10cm x 14cm.

3) All contestants must (**53**) .... the entry form printed on page 26.

4) Photographs cannot be (**54**) .... unless they are (**55**) ....

   by a stamped addressed envelope of (**56**) .... size.

5) Results will be (**57**) .... in next month's (**58**) .... of the magazine.

6) No (**59**) .... can be taken for any loss or damage to photographs.

> Remember your answers must fit the text **grammatically** and **stylistically.**

> ◀ Remember you can't use words from the first text. You need a slightly more formal expression here.

5 *For questions **60–65**, read through the following text and then choose from the list **A–J** the best phrase or sentence given below to fill each of the blanks. Write one letter **(A–J)** in each space.* **Some of the suggested answers do not fit at all.***One answer has been given as an example.*

CAR CHAOS

On the surface, Los Angeles seems to be an extremely convenient city. With hundreds of miles of freeways criss-crossing the city and its surrounding suburbs, cars can move around two or three times faster than in European cities like London. (**0**)..F...

This is because "Angelinos" also have to travel three times as far. Speed is not much of an advantage when the additional distance you have to travel soaks up the time you gain.

Los Angeles has a transport system which is extremely inefficient in its use of space and energy. Although LA has the second largest bus fleet in the US, only three per cent of journeys are made by bus. (**60**) .....

It's almost impossible to live without a car in the 'drive-in' suburbs. (**61**) ..... How would you get to the bank, the shopping mall, the school, or the office? The answer is obvious. You drive because things are so spread out that you can't do anything else.

In the inner city, there is less mobility. (**62**) ..... Many cannot drive. Others cannot afford a car. And, in any case, driving is unpleasant because of the congestion. Public transport is expensive, unless it is subsidized. (**63**) .....

The inner cities tend to be the older and more historic parts. They are now being violently disrupted to make them fit for cars. In this process people are being edged out and treated as second-class citizens. (**64**) ..... Motorways loop their way through inner cities, putting the convenience of drivers before everyone else's lives.

It is no accident that cars should have dominated North American and Australian cities so completely. (**65**) ..... Not just for motorways but also for parking, whether at home, in the city centre for office workers or by the supermarket for shoppers.

From *The New Internationalist*

Sentence 60 links with the next section. There's a clue in the word *suburbs*.

Sentence 64 provides a contrast to the previous one. The point is explained in more detail in the sentence which follows.

A And the poor can't afford high fares.

B Los Angeles has around half this figure.

C The car gets first-class treatment.

D Driving is as natural as breathing; to be carless would be almost un-American.

E Cars need vast tracts of land.

F But the *impression* of speed is all it is.

G Outside the denser inner area, bus services barely exist.

H But it is not unique.

I Here the people rely on public transport.

J Some are old and have never learnt to drive.

6 *Use the following notes from a reference book to prepare a brief fact sheet about New Zealand. Write **one complete sentence** for each numbered set of notes, using connecting words and phrases as appropriate. You may add words or change the form of words given in the notes but do not add any extra information. The first point has been expanded for you as an example.*

---

0 South east of Australia in Pacific Ocean – two large islands: North Island and South Island + smaller islands.

66 Maori name: Aotearoa "Land of the Long White Cloud"

67 North Island – most people live – fertile plains, mountain ranges and volcanic region (several active volcanoes)

68 South Island – Southern Alps form unbroken chain 650 kilometres – highest point Mount Cook (3704 metres)

69 Population: 3.3 million; Languages: English (official language), Maori

70 Capital: Wellington ("Windy City"), port southern part North Island

71 Climate: cool and temperate – max. temp. 24° C (Jan/Feb), min. 6° C (July)

72 Main exports: dairy products, wool, lamb/mutton; tourism major source income.

Remember to read the **example sentence** carefully – you can usually learn something from it! Notice here that the two islands take the definite article eg *the* North island.

Country Profile: New Zealand

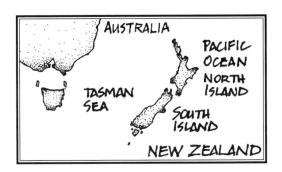

---

0 New Zealand lies to the south east of Australia in the Pacific Ocean and consists of two large islands, the North Island and the South Island, together with some smaller islands.

66

67

68

69

70

71

72

Try to use a variety of ways of linking in sentences – including **relative pronouns** like *who*, *which*, and *where*, and **conjunctions** like *and*, *but* and *while*.

Section A

*You will hear some information about three different answering machines. For questions **1–23**, complete the table by filling in the missing information or by ticking (√) the boxes to indicate what features each machine has. If a machine does not have a particular feature, put a cross (**X**). Four answers have been given as examples.*

You will hear the recording twice.

The information isn't always given in exactly the same order as the questions. Make sure you read the questions in advance so you know what to listen for.

Remember that the recording may use slightly different words from the question. Think of another way of saying "clarity of recording".

	Budgie		Cuckoo		Vulture
Max. announcement time (seconds)	30	1		2	
Max. message time (seconds)	3		4		unlimited
Logs time/date	5		√	6	
2-way recording	X	7		8	
Remote control	9		10		11
Wall-mounting	12		13		14
Clarity of recording	15		16		17
Easy to use	18		19		20
Good value for money	21		22		23

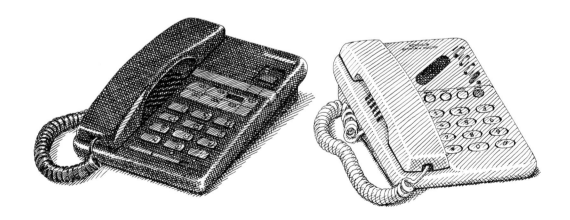

Section B

*You will hear a tour guide giving a group of tourists some extra details about their programme. As you listen, you must fill in the information for questions **24–31**.*

*Listen very carefully as you will hear this piece only **ONCE**.*

Sunday September 14th

| 18.30 | Arrival at Amman. You will be met by your tour guide. | *Name:* | **24** |
| 20.30 | ~~Welcome dinner~~ | *Hotel will provide:* | **25** |

You may be asked to spell a person's name. Listen carefully and spell what you hear. Several alternatives are usually acceptable.

Monday September 15th

	Breakfast	*served*	**26**
09.30	Coach tour of city		
	Afternoon and evening free		
		Optional visit to	**27**
		Buffet dinner with	**28**

Notice that in **questions 26, 27, 30** and **31** you can use note form answers.

Tuesday September 16th

	Breakfast	*Wear*	**29**
08.30	Coaches depart for Petra		
11.30	Tour of ancient city on horseback, followed by lunch at Petra Vista Hotel.		
16.00	Depart Petra	*Afternoon tea at*	**30**
19.00	1001 Arabian Nights Dinner		

Wednesday September 17th

	Breakfast		
10.30	Depart for airport.	*Assemble in*	**31**
12.00	Flight departs		

65

Section C

With multiple-choice questions, read through all the questions first, if possible, and try to predict the correct answers.

*You will hear part of an interview with a sub editor on a newspaper. For questions 32–38 choose the answer which you think fits best. Give **one answer only** to each question.*

You will hear the recording twice.

32 He only works on *The Australian* part-time because

    A there's no full-time work available.
    B he also works on another newspaper.
    C he prefers not to work full-time.
    D he's still learning about the job.

33 Part of his work involves

    A acting as deputy editor.
    B correcting mistakes.
    C training new reporters.
    D taking pictures for articles.

34 Why are "breakout heads" used?

    A to fill up space on the page.
    B to say what the article's about.
    C to explain what is shown in the pictures.
    D to make the page look more readable.

35 How has his work changed in recent years?

    A He has to start work earlier.
    B He has to write for other newspapers.

    C There are more editions to prepare.
    D There is more overseas material.

36 One problem the newspaper has is that

    A it doesn't have any new technology.
    B it doesn't have the latest technology.
    C editors refuse to use new technology.
    D editors aren't trained to use new technology.

37 "House ads" advertise different

    A business opportunities.
    B types of accommodation.
    C sections of the newspaper.
    D newspapers in the same group.

38 In its attitude to headlines, he seems to find his newspaper

    A a bit too serious.
    B in bad taste.
    C completely dishonest.
    D admirable.

Beware "all or nothing" answers as in **question 38** – answers with the words "completely", "never", "always", etc. They often say more than is really true.

Section D

You · will hear five people talking about publications they read.
You will hear the recording twice.

Task One

*Letters **A–H** list different types of publication. As you listen, decide which one on the list each speaker is referring to. For questions **39–43**, put the letter of the publication against the appropriate speaker.*

A a local newspaper

B a national daily newspaper

C a children's comic

D a music magazine

E a trade or professional journal

F a TV guide

G a humorous magazine

H a Sunday newspaper

SPEAKER 1	39
SPEAKER 2	40
SPEAKER 3	41
SPEAKER 4	42
SPEAKER 5	43

> Remember that the answer may not be directly stated on the tape. Listen for clues in what the speakers say about the publications they read.

Task Two

*Letters **A–H** list some of the positive features of the different publications which the speakers mention. As you listen, indicate which **two** features are mentioned by each speaker.*

A good value

B free

C horoscopes

D competitions

E advertisements

F sport

G reader's letters

H detailed articles

SPEAKER 1	44	45	
SPEAKER 2	46	47	
SPEAKER 3	48	49	
SPEAKER 4	50	51	
SPEAKER 5	52	53	

> Remember that the information you hear on the tape may be expressed slightly differently from the question. The speakers use different ways of saying something is "free" or "good value".

Work with another student.

Phase A

(about 3 minutes)

- Introduce yourselves to each other.
- Find out where your partner lives and how he/she feels about that place. Give your partner the same information about yourself.
- Tell your partner about a good friend of yours. Ask your partner about their friends.
- Find out what kind of physical exercise your partner takes. Explain what exercise you take.

| Remember to ask these questions in **you own words**, as naturally as possible. |

| Really **listen** to what your partner has to say and ask some follow-up questions, if possible. |

Phase B

(3 or 4 minutes)

Task 1 (Describe and identify)

Candidate A has six pictures. Candidate B has the same pictures but in a different order and also an extra one. Don't look at each other's pictures.

Candidate A: Turn to the set of pictures on page 147 and describe them clearly so that your partner can identify them.

Candidate B: Turn to the set of pictures on page 148. Listen to your partner's description and decide which picture is not described. You may make notes if you wish. When A has finished, describe the remaining picture.

| Remember Candidate A should aim to talk for about **a minute**, without interruption. |

Task 2 (Spot the difference)

You will each have a picture to look at. The pictures are similar but not the same. Don't look at each other's pictures.

Candidate B: Turn to the picture on page 138 and describe what you can see.
You have about a minute.

Candidate A: Turn to the picture on page 137 and listen to your partner's description. You can make notes on a piece of paper if you wish. When B has finished, mention any differences you have noted. Do you know where the picture might have been taken?
Now compare the two pictures.

| Try to express a **personal reaction** to what you see. How would you describe the style of the room? Would you like to live there? |

68

Phase C

(3 or 4 minutes)

You have both won a competition run by a company which specialises in new and slightly unusual products. As a prize, you can choose any of the items from the company's catalogue shown on page 144.

Discuss with your partner how useful you consider each item to be. Explain which one you would choose as your prize. It could be for yourself, as a present for a friend, or even as a present for someone you don't like! Find out what your partner would choose, and why.

> Remember to give your partner an equal opportunity to speak and to really **listen** to what he/she says.

Phase D

(3 or 4 minutes)

In this phase the examiner would ask you to report which items you have chosen from the catalogue and then ask a few more questions to continue the discussion.

To practise your reporting skills, work with another pair and take it in turns to summarise and explain the conclusions you reached.

> You'll need to **summarise** your discussions and explain the **reasons** for your decisions.

PRACTICE TEST

3

Answer **all** questions

First text/questions 1–20

Answer questions **1–20** by referring to the newspaper article called "Cruising" on page **71.**

Questions **1–20** ask you about the ships or the cruises on those ships which are mentioned in the text. Answer each question by choosing from the list **A–E**.

Note: When more than one answer is required, these may be given **in any order.**

Questions 1–6 are rapid skimming questions. You can find the information at the beginning of each section. Don't read any further at this stage.

Which ship was built most recently?	**1**	**A**	Norway
Which ship has the largest crew?	**2**	**B**	Queen Elizabeth II
Which ship has the fewest passengers?	**3**	**C**	Royal Princess
Which is the biggest ship?	**4**	**D**	Royal Viking Sun
Which cruise lasts longest?	**5**	**E**	Sagafjord
Which cruise has the cheapest fare?	**6**		

Which cruise would be most suitable for

older people?	**7**	**8** ....
people with children?	**9**	
people interested in photography?	**10**	
people interested in golf?	**11**	
people interested in shopping?	**12**........	**13** ....

Questions 7–13: Look out for different ways of expressing these ideas in the text.

Which ship was considered most comfortable to travel in?	**14**	
Which ship has an excellent library?	**15**	
On which cruise were the tours specially recommended?	**16**	
On which cruise are you likely to see whales?	**17**	**18** ....
Which cruise had the best entertainment?	**19**	
Which cruise had the worst restaurant service?	**20**	

70

Cruising

COMPARING THE OPTIONS

Our aim was to compare facilities, style, route and prices on a variety of cruises. We award marks out of 10.

THE BIG SHIPS

A NORWAY: *1,035ft long; 75,000 tons; 2,044 passengers; built 1961. Norwegian officers, international crew (800 in total). Cruise: Caribbean (Miami – Miami;) 7 days. £965 – £3,485.*
They don't come any bigger. Always the longest and, after a recent refit, the heaviest, but mercifully not the most passenger-intensive. It's easy to get lost among three-football-pitch-long corridors; if you forget your sunglasses it could be a 10-minute hike back to the cabin.

There are 12 cabin categories, all bright and cheerful, including four-berth family versions. This is an ideal family cruise, with lots of activities for toddlers and teenagers, and big discounts. Adult entertainment includes Los Vegas-style evening shows.

Dining is in two restaurants, or queues for hamburgers 'n' fries on deck.

The route is standard Caribbean. Lots of shopping at St John's, St Thomas and St Maarten, swimming and barbecuing on Norwegian Cruise Line's private Bahamian island.

Rating: cabins 8; service 8; food 2; entertainment 10; excursions 5; route 2. **Atmosphere:** youngish, American, families.

B QUEEN ELIZABETH II: *963ft long; 66,451 tons; 1,870 passengers; built 1969. Officers: British; crew: British/international (1,015). Cruise: Transatlantic (Southampton – New York); 5 days (each way). £1,100 – £2,430 sea (both ways).*
Unless you are exceptionally lucky, this won't be a sunshine cruise but the ship is well-prepared to amuse her customers in bad weather, with two indoor swimming pools as well as three on deck, a shopping concourse featuring Harrods, Burberry and Aquascutum, good lectures, heavy leather armchairs and the best ship's library afloat.

Cabins vary enormously, with 22 grades. It's important to realise that the dining goes with the cabin grade. Only the very top get to the admirable Princess and Queen's Grills; the so-called "First Class" get the Columbia restaurant and the rest mass catering in the Mauretania.

Rating: cabins 2–8 depending on grade; service 7; food 4-10 depending on grade; entertainment 8; lectures 9; **Atmosphere:** stately as a galleon. **High-spot:** arrival in New York.

THE MEDIUM SHIPS

C ROYAL PRINCESS: *761ft long, 44,348 tons, 1,260 passengers, built 1984. British officers, international crew (500). Cruise: The Northern Capitals (The Baltic Sea); 12 days. £1,745 – £4,920.*
An easy ship to find your way around. I particularly liked the deck area, with a choice of three swimming pools and four spa baths.

All cabins are well fitted, most have baths and are outside; those with verandahs are as splendid as any afloat. The interior features attractive paintings from a well-chosen modern art collection.

Lectures were well-researched and there was a commentary from the captain during the most interesting passages, and for whale-spotting. Dinner is better than most mass-catering and the breakfast and lunch buffets are outstanding.

The Baltic is popular cruising ground and for a whistle-stop tour of some of the most interesting cities in Europe, it's hard to beat. Good tours were arranged in every port but none of them is essential unless you can't use your legs.

Rating: cabins 5–9; service 8; food 5 in dining room, 8 in buffet; entertainment 9; route 10. **Atmosphere:** jolly, middle-aged.

High spots: Copenhagen, Stockholm, St Petersburg, Amsterdam.

D ROYAL VIKING SUN: *673ft long; 36,845 tons, 740 passengers; built 1972; Norwegian officers, Scandinavian crew (460). Cruise: New York, New England, St Lawrence river to Montreal and back to New York; 14 days. £2,271 (inside cabin) to £7,300 (suite).*

This is a ship unique in combining luxury with considerable size. If you come into this spending bracket, you can hardly fault her. She is certainly the smoothest, quietest ship I sampled, the food in the dining room, and particularly in the Garden Room Buffet, is outstanding, and the public rooms are spacious and comfortable. All the cabins have walk-in cupboards and full-size bathrooms, many have verandahs: you could be in a very exclusive hotel.

Deck space is generous – no need to reserve your space before breakfast – and you can actually do more than three strokes at a time in the swimming pool (very unusual). A unique feature is the golf simulator where a professional gives advice on shots directed at a screen.

The Sun is a very popular ship and aims to please all tastes. There are classical music concerts and also bingo and a casino; evening entertainment and lectures were disappointing.

Rating: cabins 9; service 10; food 9 for restaurant, 10 for buffet; entertainment 4; excursions 5. **Atmosphere:** sophisticated. **High spots:** Boston, Quebec, Montreal, Newport.

E SAGAFJORD: *619ft long, 24,474 tons; 620 passengers, built 1965. Norwegian officers, international crew (350). Cruise: Alaska (Vancouver to Anchorage); 13 days. £2,195 inside double, to £6,840 for penthouse suite.*

This is the second most popular cruise route in the world and the long cruise is more than justified by the never-failing excitement of scenery and wildlife. Leave the deck and binoculars for a meal, or to fetch sunglasses (you'll need them), and you miss a bear, a whale, a glacier and another stupendous photo-opportunity.

Cabins are pleasantly pastel, mostly with baths, and there is the obligatory gym and sauna. Cold weather provisions include an indoor swimming pool and lots of blankets to wrap round frozen legs. A unique feature is the local retired ladies who give daily lectures on their home grounds. Our lecture was better and more inspiring than most given by professionals.

This is one route where excursions are essential. There are 64 options. To go so far and miss the helicopter landing on the glacier or the White Pass railway ride into the Yukon would be a shame.

Rating: cabin 8; service 2 in dining room and decks (long waits, poor wine service), 8 in cabins; food: 5 restaurant, 7 Lido buffet; entertainment 5; lectures 10; route 10. **Atmosphere:** enthusiastic, middle-aged. **High-spots:** Hubbard and College glaciers.

From *The Sunday Times*

Second text/questions 21–26

For questions **21–26** you must choose which of the paragraphs **A–G** match the numbered gaps in the newspaper article. There is one extra paragraph which does not belong in any of the gaps.

PRINCE OF WHALES

Once hunted to the edge of extinction, the sperm whale is bringing new life to an ocean community which preyed on them

By Robin Eggar

The history of Kaikoura, on New Zealand's South Island, is inextricably bound with that of the whale. It owes its very creation and continuing existence to these beautiful creatures. The town was built on slaughtered whales; on whale-bone, blubber and sperm oil - and nearly died with the creatures it preyed on.

21

Whaling lingered on – in 1963, 248 sperm whales were killed - until the bottom fell out of the market. In 1978, New Zealand outlawed the killing of any marine mammal, whales, dolphins and seals, in her waters.

22

In 1988, local fisherman Roger Sutherland, his American wife Barbara Todd and the Maori-financed Kaikoura Tours started to explore the commercial viability of whale watching. In just four years the whole atmosphere of the town has been transformed. Now the very creature Kaikoura preyed on has given it a new lease of life. For it is the only place on earth where one can watch sperm whales so close at hand. Where once the boats sailed forth to kill, they now ferry out the tourists to marvel, watch and wonder.

23

The seas around Kaikoura are a marine wonderland, teeming with crayfish and groper, and colonies of seals. On this planet there are 76 species of whale and dolphin, 15 of which can be seen regularly in Kaikoura waters.

24

While young males tend to move about individually or in pairs, lucky visitors occasionally see something special. "I had 15 whales all in a line for about 15 minutes once," says Richard Oliver, Kaikoura sea operations manager and expert at locating whales with a hydrophone (underwater microphone).

Although some whales can be playful, they generally stay aloof. "They tolerate us for their own pleasure and perhaps curiosity," says Richard. "They have minds of their own, different temperaments and there are a couple I completely trust. Being out there on the ocean with them is an awe-inspiring thing."

25

An unknown author once wrote: Whatever that ancient chemistry of gentle change that produced great whales, it will never again be duplicated in the lifetime of this planet. If we allow the extinction of whales, we and they will never have another chance."

26

A Although primarily appealing to young, backpacking eco-tourists, whale-watching has caught the public imagination. Last year 40,000 people took the £27 three-hour trip, with a subsequent knock-on effect for the local economy. Hotel occupancy is up from 15 per cent to 96 per cent in four years, while property prices are rising faster than anywhere in New Zealand.

B Perhaps they are better at forgiveness than we are. Playful humpback whales are returning to Kaikoura waters. Absent for the past 25 years, they have been sighted in increasing numbers for the past two Julys. But it may not be enough. Some nations have chosen to abandon the international ban on commercial whaling and so threaten the world's whales.

C The whales have given the town of Kaikoura another chance. Surely, we owe them the same?

D By then the whales had long been forgotten, except in the folk memory of fishermen and Maori story-tellers. Kaikoura slid into slow, seemingly irreversible decline. Until someone remembered the whales.

E As the whale sinks into the trough between the waves, he exhales a snow-white spray from his blow-hole. For 10 minutes the ritual continues until, accompanied by sighs of disappointment, the body vanishes beneath the water.

F This remarkable abundance is all down to a trick of geology and geography. Less than a mile offshore the continental shelf drops into deep-water canyons just where a warm southbound current converges with a cold northerly one. This produces a thriving food chain and ideal conditions for young male sperm whales, who spend their adolescent years, from 13 to 25, there until they are mature enough to breed.

G A Maori legend tells of Paikea who first rode into South Bay on the back of Tohora, a giant whale. Then came the pakeha (white man) with their harpoons, men like Scot George Fyffe who established a whaling station in 1842. When it closed 80 years later, the whales were close to extinct.

From *The Sunday Mirror Magazine*

Question 22: There are two clues, one in the section before (In 1978...) and one in the section following (*Roger Sutherland...*) Look for a paragraph which links these two points.

Question 24: the section before talks about how many species can be seen. The missing section refers to this and also has a direct link with the next paragraph.

Third text/questions 27–32

Read the newspaper article below and then answer the questions on page 75.

Classrooms with the writing on the wall

Maintaining classroom discipline is a growing problem for many schools. Some children seem incapable of following the rules, perhaps because they feel they are unreasonable or unclear.

There can be no such excuses at Bebington High School on the Wirral. When children misbehave at Bebington, the teacher immediately writes their names on the classroom blackboard. They know they are in trouble and they know what the penalty is likely to be. Their classmates know too that the choice to break the rules was their own.

The effect, claim the proponents of this American system of discipline, has been to improve behaviour, allowing more time to be spent on teaching. "Assertive discipline" was introduced into Bebington last September and Margaret Hodson, a science teacher, says the results are "little short of a miracle"

Since the programme was introduced into England two years ago, 450 schools, 80 per cent of them primary have adopted the scheme. Whether the programme spreads more widely depends to some extent on the government's attitude. Adrian Smith, of Behaviour Management, the Bristol-based company marketing the scheme in Brian, will this week meet Eric Forth, the Junior Schools Minister, to tell him of the benefits achieved by schools using the programme.

Bebington, a 1,000-pupil 11–to–18 secondary modern school, was always considered good for a school of its type, but staff claim that standards of behaviour increased dramatically last term, with an improvement in the work rate of the children and less stress on the teachers.

The basis of the programme, which costs schools £22 a day for each person trained, is that all children have a right to choose how they behave but they must face the consequences of that choice. A set of straightforward rules is displayed on a wall in each classroom, together with a set of rewards and consequences.

The rules at Bebington are: arrive on time to lessons and enter the room quietly; remain in your seat unless asked to move; come to lessons properly equipped; listen

No excuses: Lesley Anne McFeat at work at Bebington

to and follow instructions the first time they are given; raise your hand before answering or speaking; and treat others, their work and equipment with respect.

Pupils who behave well during a lesson are rewarded with an "R" mark in the teacher's record book. Six Rs win them a "bronze" letter of commendation to take home to their parents. Twelve "Rs" bring a silver letter, 18 a gold, and 24 a diploma of excellence presented by the head teacher at assembly. Diploma winners are then able to choose a special award in negotiation with the staff, such as a non-uniform day or a trip out.

Teachers can also award a certificate of merit for individual pieces of good work or behaviour or for long-term excellent punctuality or attendance. All letters and certificates earned by the pupils are eventually kept in their record of achievement, available to potential employers.

Paul Shryane, the deputy head at Bebington, who first suggested that the scheme be adopted, says that rewarding good behaviour makes children focus on the benefits of concentrating on work and creates a positive environment for classroom work.

The sanctions open to teachers for pupils who break the rules are: detention of five minutes, 15 minutes or 30 minutes at lunchtime with the parents informed. The ultimate sanction before being excluded is being sent to the academic remove, where children are isolated from the rest of the school for periods ranging from one lesson to a whole day. They are continually supervised by a member of the staff and their parents are invited to the school to discuss their child's behaviour.

Assertive discipline allows the staff to deal quickly with disruptive pupils: children can see the consequence of their action on the wall. As a result, the time spent on teaching in the classroom is up substantially, says John Adamson, a modern languages teacher at the school. He estimates that the curriculum was covered 25 per cent more quickly last term than in previous years.

In adapting the scheme for British use, the Bebington staff, who all agreed that it was the right move for their school, had to revise the rewards system, which in American schools tends to be material. Offers of sweets or gifts for good behaviour were deemed inappropriate.

Mr Shryane says: "Much assertive discipline is based on sound traditional educational practice. What is new is the formalised consistency of a whole school approach, and the consistent rewarding of those who achieve the standards asked of them."

Put rather more controversially, society has moved on, it seems, from the time where the teacher could expect good behaviour from the majority of pupils as a matter of course. Now they have to reward it.

DAVID TYTLER

From *The Times*

27 What are the results of the new system at Bebington High School?

    A   It's too early to say.

    B   Disappointing so far.

    C   Fairly promising.

    D   Very encouraging.

28 How many schools have adopted the new scheme?

    A   Most primary schools.

    B   More primary schools than secondary schools.

    C   A few experimental schools.

    D   Only schools nominated by the government.

> Beware of options which contain words which are the same as, or similar to, words in the text. They may not mean exactly the same thing.

29 What is the key feature of the new system?

    A   Children learn to take responsibility for their actions.

    B   Children have to be punctual for all their lessons.

    C   Badly-behaved children are made to feel ashamed.

    D   Well-behaved children are awarded with medals.

30 What happens to children who continue to behave badly?

    A   They are sent home.

    B   Their parents are asked to discipline them.

    C   They are kept away from other pupils for a time.

    D   They have to miss lunch.

31 How does the scheme in Britain compare with the American one?

    A   The rules are stricter.

    B   The punishments are less severe.

    C   The rewards are different.

    D   It's exactly the same.

> Beware of "all-or-nothing" options which may say more than is actually true.

32 What seems to be the writer's view of the subject?

    A   The system is more suitable for America than Britain.

    B   It's a pity good behaviour can't be taken for granted any more.

    C   Children who behave badly should be helped, not punished.

    D   It's a controversial idea and only time will tell if it's successful.

Fourth text/questions 33 – 51

Answer questions 33–51 by referring to the article on children's competitions on page 77.

For questions 33–51 answer by choosing from the sections of the article A–K on page 77.
Note: When more than one answer is required, you may give the answers in any order.

For which competition or competitions do you have to

buy some food?	33		
read a comic or magazine?	34	35	36 ......
	37		
watch television?	38	39	
go to a post office?	40		

In which competition or competitions could you win

a holiday abroad?	41	42 ......
a book?	43	
sweets?	44	
make-up?	45	
money?	46	

Which competition or competitions would be suitable for

animal lovers?	47		
artistic children?	48	49	50 ......
children of 12 years old?	51		

Like many of these questions, **44** and **45** use **general** terms. You need to look for **specific** examples in the text.

How to win prizes for keeping quiet

Finding it difficult to keep the children amused during the long, dark evenings?
The answer, **Jane Bidder** *says, is to get them hooked on competitions*

The chance of winning something for nothing, apart from a little know-how, is always attractive, and provides an opportunity for children to prove their artistic or verbal skills.

Below (with the help of my three children), I have tracked down the most exciting competitions for tinies through to teenagers. So now is the time to sharpen their pencils and your wits and get cracking on a competition that could bring a worthwhile prize.

A **Artistic writers** can show off their calligraphic skills with the Osmiroid Spirit of the Letter Competition, run by Berol. There are four entry classes, from designing a small poster to producing a notice for a nature trail. Prizes include a calligraphic weekend and equipment. Closing date May 31 1993. Age ten upwards. Entry forms from Berol, Oldmeadow Road, Kings Lynn, Norfolk PE30 4JR.

B **Babies** too young for most competitions can pose for a photograph to enter Mothercare's happy faces competition in either the 0–18 months category, or 18 months to five years. Running in selected stores throughout Britain, the competition prizes include a family holiday for four to Euro Disney in Paris, video camcorders and vouchers. Ring Paintbox Portraits on 0722 412202 to find your nearest store competition.

C **Colour** a pantomime scene in Snap magazine (December issue) and win a Sega Master system, or one of 20 mystery Christmas stockings for runners-up (closing date December 14). Or, in the same issue, answer a simple question about a children's illustrator and win one of 20 chocolate selection stockings plus party tapes. Or again, complete a sentence about Disney's *Basil the Great Mouse*

Detective and win one of five videos. Closing date for these two competitions is December 20.

D **Canny comp:** Enter the Heinz Spaghetti competition by filling in the prize draw form (inside the label) to win one of 1,000 Sega Master Systems II (are we the only family not to have one?). Closing date November 27.

E **Young writers:** Look out for the Royal Mail Young Letter Writer competition – leaflets available in most offices at the begin-

> *What better confidence booster than for a child to be able to cry, 'I've won'?*

ning of January. The theme is still to be decided: last year's subject was anything "green". Prizes range from £100 for regional winners to £400 for national winners. Closing date: first week in April.

F **Family holiday:** Parents would be delighted if a child won a week's holiday in Boston, USA, for a family of four – the first prize in Harrods Freedom Trail in-store competition. The competition starts on December 14, when Father Christmas arrives (free admission to grotto) and ends December 24. Entrants (under the age of 12) have to answer questions on New England landmarks.

G **Camera caper:** Prove your photographic skills by taking a photograph (with your own camera or someone else's) and win a trip

to the Wimbledon tennis next summer by joining the Halifax Building Society LittleXtra Club. Other competitions, detailed in the free club magazine, include identifying three road signs to win a Corgi garage, and completing a puzzle to pocket one of 30 *Where's Wally?* videos. Open to children under 11. Closing date for all entries is March 29. Children can join the clubs at any Halifax branch by opening an account.

H **Scribble a few lines** about yourself and send in your picture to *Mandy & Judy* comic for its Reader of the Week competition. The winner receives a range of Polly Pocket Pretty Me cosmetics.

I **Telly addicts** can win prizes every Sunday morning by watching BBC's *But First This* programme for children, 7.30am–12pm.

J **Under six year olds** can design a Christmas picture in any medium and win Bluebird toys, including Jumbo Fun Plane, Big Red Fun Bus, Big Yellow Teapot, with teasets and lunchboxes for runners up. Watch Children's Channel on satellite/cable TV (8.45–10.45am and 1–3pm)

K **Adopt a chimp** by answering a true/false question about chimpanzees in the Woolwich Building Society's Kids Club magazine (details below). You can then be the official adoptive owner of a four-legged pet at the Chimp Rescue Centre in Wareham, Dorset. Less zoo-minded readers might prefer tamer prizes from the Woolwich, such as *The Guinness Book of Records* (answer multiple choice questions) or a board game (spot the odd one out). Entry forms are in the company magazine, which is sent to you after opening an account for £1. Under-12s only.

> If you don't know a word (like *chimp*), look for any **extra information** in the text which might help explain the meaning.

Instructions to candidates

*This paper contains one Section A task and four Section B tasks. You must complete the Section A task and **one** task from Section B.*

The two sections carry equal marks.

*Read the instructions and consider the information **carefully** both for section A and the task you select for Section B.*

Section A

1   You are planning to spend two weeks in Sydney, Australia, where some friends of yours are now living. They haven't got room to put you up and you would prefer to stay in a rented apartment rather than a hotel. Another friend, who has visited Sydney, has sent you a brochure for a company which seems to offer suitable accommodation, and you have made a few notes on it.

There's a lot of information to digest here so it's more important than ever to highlight the key points.

▶ Read the brochure and the notes you have made on it, the extract from your friend's letter and then, **using the information carefully,** write the letter and note described in the instructions on page 79.

FORGET SUPER-EXPENSIVE HOTELS ... BE INDEPENDENT AND STAY IN STYLE.

Star Point Holiday Units now offers you the City's biggest selection of short-term accommodation.

* FULLY FURNISHED
* CONVENIENT LOCATIONS
* FLEXIBLE BOOKINGS   *what is this exactly?*
* BEST PRICES
* EASY PARKING

We have excellent accommodation in most areas of Sydney and can usually place you close to where your friends or family live or just minutes away from the city's many tourist districts. Tell us the reason for your visit and we'll make sure you are conveniently located.

Star Point Holiday Units are completely self-contained and furnished to a high standard. All our apartme ts are fully equipped with colour television, linen, crockery and kitchen needs.

iron? hair dryer! laundry facilities?

A telephone is installed in each apartment and **all your local calls are free of charge!**

how are international calls charged?

Star Point Holiday Units are just as accommodating as a hotel but with more reasonable rates and greater privacy. The period of rental is as flexible as you like. Book on a daily, weekly or monthly basis. If you happen to be looking for an economical alternative there are often apartments, such as those without a harbour view, which are available at lower rates.

Example Rental Fees (Daily)   *weekly rates?*

Apartment Category	Harbour View	Other Outlook
Studio	$ 55 - 65	$45 - 55
1 Bedroom	$ 65 - 75	$55 - 65
2 Bedroom	$ 85 - 100	$75 - 85

WE WILL NEED TO KNOW   *deposit required?*
* Commencement date   *10-25 Aug*
* Anticipated last day
* How many people will be staying   *near Bondi*
* How large an apartment you need   *Beach*
* Which area of the city you would prefer   *if pos*

STAR POINT HOLIDAY UNITS

Postal Address: PO Box 400
North Sydney, NSW 1000, Australia

I enclose a brochure for rented apartments which I picked up when I was in Sydney last year. The prices aren't exactly cheap (and they may be slightly out of date now) but I imagine weekly rates are cheaper than the daily ones quoted. As you're on your own, you could opt for a "Studio" (which must mean some kind of bed-sitter, I suppose) and I'm sure you could manage without a harbour view. It would be much nicer to have your own place to stay in and you'd save a lot by being able to cook for yourself rather than eat in restaurants. Why not write to the company and check on a few details? Hope this helps. Let me know how you get on.

Write (a) a suitable **letter of enquiry** to Star Point Holiday Units giving details of the type of accommodation you are interested in and when you would require it, and asking for the extra information you need. (approximately 200 words)

You must lay out the letter in the appropriate way but it is not necessary to include addresses.

(b) a **note** to your friend, thanking them for the information and advice, and telling them briefly what you have done. (approximately 50 words)

> Make sure you answer both parts of the question – you'll lose a lot of marks if you don't write the note.

Section B

*Choose **ONE** of the following writing tasks. Your answer should follow exactly the instructions given. Write approximately 250 words.*

2   Some British friends of yours are planning to spend three weeks in the summer touring your country by car. This will be their first visit to your country and they have written to ask you to suggest a route they could take and some places they should particularly visit. Write a **detailed note**, suggesting two or three possible routes and mentioning the advantages and drawbacks of each choice.

> See the guidelines in Test 1 (page 10) for writing a detailed note. Make sure you mention the advantages and disadvantages of each route.

3   This letter has appeared in a local English language magazine.

Sir,
Why is our television so awful these days? There seems to be nothing but violence, mindless gameshows or tired old American comedies. I look in vain for anything of educational value, originality or genuine artistic merit. I'm afraid to let my children watch television alone for fear of the damaging effect some of the more violent dramas may have on them. I have now decided to get rid of our TV set and I suggest other readers do the same.

Yours faithfully,
MICHAEL BROWN

> Notice that you don't necessarily think that Michael Brown is totally wrong in his views. Your article should aim to offer a more balanced argument.

You think the writer has exaggerated the problems and failed to mention a number of very worthwhile programmes. Write a short **article** expressing your views for the "Personal Opinion" section of the magazine.

Your instructions can be in the form of a note, with a brief introduction explaining the problem. The key thing is to make sure your instructions are totally clear to your friend.

4 Unfortunately you forgot to reconfirm your return flight from a holiday destination and, as a result, you find there are no seats available. The airline has now told you that the earliest you can travel is in four days' time. This is a problem because there are a number of things which need to be done at home and there are also important arrangements which need to be cancelled or changed. The only solution is to send a fax to a friend who has a key to your house/flat and who can probably sort out the main problems for you. Write a suitable **set of instructions** for your friend.

This gives you the opportunity to tell an interesting story. The account can be in the form of a report (no need for subheadings) or a letter. Imagine you really want the child to win the award.

5 An international children's society offers annual awards to children who have shown examples of great bravery. Candidates for the award have to be nominated by a relative or friend who must submit a detailed account of the circumstances involved. Write an **account** for the society, describing the child you wish to nominate, explaining exactly what happened, and saying why you think they deserve to win an award.

Answer **all** questions.

1 *For questions **1–15**, read the article below and circle the letter next to the word which best fits each space. The exercise begins with an example* **(0)**.

Talking rubbish

Lasanda Kurukulasuriya *takes a Sri Lankan view of recycling*

Reduce! Re-use! Recycle! The message hits Canadian **(0)** ....consumers.... through all the media. As newcomers from Sri Lanka, we compare the situation here with the one back home. We may not be the most environmentally **(1)** .... citizens in the world but, compared with this, we do not have a rubbish problem – yet.

Like many shoppers in Colombo, my partner Shahid and I used to have a cane basket we **(2)** .... with us to the Sunday market or *pola* every week. No environmentalist could have **(3)** .... about it. You need a good strong basket at the *pola*. There are no supermarket **(4)** .... to push around. Most items – rice, flour, vegetables, fruit, biscuits, eggs – are bought **(5)** .... or wrapped in newspaper. At **(6)** .... we would carry one plastic bag separately. For eggs we took a reusable plastic tray with us.

When income **(7)** .... are low, people need to buy in small quantities. It is quite normal to ask for a **(8)** .... envelope, two eggs or 100 grams of sugar. The **(9)** .... is that, for the most part, urban consumers in Sri Lanka cannot *afford* the luxury of waste. Most people do not buy more from the grocers than they know they will actually consume. They re-use whatever they can and are loath to discard bags, jars, tins or boxes that can be **(10)** .... to other uses.

But in recent years Western-style supermarkets have begun to spring up in Colombo. They hold out the **(11)** .... of a clean, efficient, streamlined service to customers. A **(12)** .... of imported goods, dressed up in their layers of attractive, colourful **(13)** .... beckons from the shelves. These are the **(14)** .... products that demand your attention on the TV advertisements. **(15)** .... with them, Sri Lanka, like so many other developing countries, may have imported a problem that once never existed.

From The New Internationalist

> **Question 3:**
> think only about **grammar**! Only one of these verbs takes *about* as a preposition.

	A	B	C	D
0	A customers	(B) consumers	C clients	D buyers
1	A qualified	B concerned	C worried	D experienced
2	A took over	B took away	C took along	D took up
3	A complained	B criticised	C disapproved	D accused
4	A wheelbarrows	B wagons	C trolleys	D carriages
5	A free	B in pieces	C bit by bit	D loose
6	A maximum	B most	C highest	D best
7	A rates	B amounts	C sizes	D levels
8	A simple	B singular	C single	D sole
9	A point	B case	C example	D question
10	A made	B set	C given	D put
11	A promise	B advantage	C evidence	D sight
12	A set	B range	C store	D band
13	A packets	B packs	C packaging	D padding
14	A very	B just	C similar	D likely
15	A In addition	B As well	C Among	D Along

Remember you need exactly the right word for the **context.** After you've finished this test, use a dictionary to check how each of these words is used.

2 For questions **1–30,** complete the following article by writing the missing words in the spaces provided. **Use only one word for each space.** The exercise begins with an example (**0**).

New £20 note to prevent forgeries

THE CENTRAL BANK (**0**) .....has..... had to introduce a new £20 note to prevent (**16**) .... unintended "privatisation" of the note printing business by forgers, the Governor of the Central Bank, Mr Maurice Doyle, said when he unveiled the note in Dublin yesterday. It is (**17**) .... introduced to combat the increasing banknote forgery which has come about in recent years as a result of developments (**18**) .... photocopying and printing, he said. (**19**) .... with access to a high quality colour photocopier and the correct paper (**20**) .... make a copy of the old £20 note that was good enough to (**21**) .... passed unnoticed (**22**) .... a crowded shop counter, he said. Although forgery problems in Ireland are not comparable (**23**) .... those of the major international currencies, such as the dollar, the Irish £20 note has some "close cousins" said Mr Doyle.

The new note, which comes (**24**) .... circulation on Monday, incorporates several features that will (**25**) .... it harder to forge. It has a watermark incorporating the number 20 and a silver security thread which shows when the note is held up to the light. It also incorporates a hidden image of the letters IR, which can only be (**26**) .... when the note is tilted towards the light, and microprinting (**27**) .... the front and reverse. The note also contains features that will enable visually impaired people to recognise it. They include a mark that can be felt (**28**) .... the fingertips. (**29**) .... note in the new series will be (**30**) .... a different size and be printed on different paper to give it a different "feel".

From *The Irish Times*

Question 20: check the **tense** by looking at the whole sentence. Notice that this is an example of reported speech.

Section B

3 *In the following advertisement for a guide to travelling as an air courier all the full stops (.) and question marks (?) have been removed. Show where the full-stops (.) or question marks (?) should be inserted by writing them, together with the preceding word, in the spaces provided. Some lines are correct. Indicate these lines with a tick (√). The exercise begins with two examples (0).*

> Remember to read the **instructions** very carefully. Here you need to write the word before the punctuation mark.

TRAVEL FREE AS AN AIR COURIER

Did you know that there are people quietly paying less than 10%   0 ....√.........

for their air travel some are holidaying with friends in the States for   0 ...travel?.....

as little as £25 while others travel absolutely free, apart from a small   31 ....

registration fee how would you like to visit Paris, New York, Hong   32 ....

Kong or Tokyo, to name but a few, for a fraction of the normal price   33 ....

these are return fares with no extras and they're all scheduled   34 ....

flights with the best of the major world airlines how can you secure   35 ....

these incredible discounts for yourself simply by flying as a   36 ....

freelance air courier with one of the major international package   37 ....

and parcel distributors being an air courier is easy, convenient,   38 ....

fun and rewarding anyone can register as a courier, no matter   39 ....

what they do for a living you will act on a part-time basis and it's   40 ....

entirely up to you to choose where you want to go, when and how   41 ....

often it's ideal if you're in business, retired, a student, a charity   42 ....

volunteer, or if you just want to get away from it all before you book   43 ....

your next break and pay over the odds yet again, discover the   44 ....

secrets to air courier travel and fly the world at huge savings to   45 ....

claim your copy of this invaluable guide, simply complete and

return the coupon below.

> Remember to read through the whole text first, to get a general picture, before you think about the punctuation in detail.

4 *For questions 46–60, read the following informal note about a meeting and use the information to complete the numbered gaps in the formal letter. **Use no more than two words** for each gap. The exercise begins with an example (0). The words you need **do not occur** in the informal note.*

Dear Debbie,

Just a note to let you know that I can't come to the AGM next Thurs. Sorry about this – I've got to go down to my mother's and sort out some problems.

You did say that if I couldn't make the meeting, you wouldn't mind standing in for me and I trust this is still OK. It's basically just a question of taking notes and saying a few words about the conference we organised in the summer.

I'll let the Chair know what we've arranged and I'll also mention my feelings about a couple of the items on the agenda. As you know, I'm dead against the idea of bumping up the annual membership fee for next year - I think we'd just lose members. On the other hand, I've no objection to bringing in a rule to stop people smoking at meetings.

Many thanks for helping out in this way.

Yours

Notice that the **style** is very formal and that you will need to use some special expressions connected with the topic of meetings/committees.

Dear Madam Chair,

I (**0**)......*regret*...... to inform you that I will be (**46**)................... to (**47**)....................... the Annual General Meeting which is to (**48**).................. on Thursday 27th., owing to the fact that I have some urgent family (**49**)................... to deal with.

My colleague, Deborah Brandon, has kindly (**50**).................. to take my (**51**) .... at the meeting and to give a brief (**52**) .... on the summer conference.

I should like to take this (**53**)................. to comment on two of the agenda items. Firstly, I do not (**54**)................. the proposal to (**55**)................. the membership fee for the coming year. It (**56**)................. me that such a move would certainly (**57**)............... a (**58**)................. in membership numbers. I am, however, fully (**59**)................. of the move to (**60**).................. a ban on smoking at meetings.

Yours sincerely,

Section B

5   *For questions **61–66**, read through the following text and then choose from the list **A–J** the best phrase or sentence given below to fill each of the blanks. Write one letter (**A–J**) in each space.* **Some of the suggested answers do not fit at all.** *One answer has been given as an example (**0**).*

Book reading a lost art at Harvard

From Charles Bremner, New York

Question 61:
the clue is in *survey* – do you think the results of this survey are likely to have pleased or saddened the professor?

Question 64:
the clue is in the following sentence, which seems to be correcting a possible wrong impression.

Hardly a day goes by without a fresh demonstration of the ignorance of America's first video generation. Illiteracy is growing, and a new poll shows that a quarter of university students have no idea when Columbus reached America, leading pessimistic academics to prophesy a new barbarism.

Some institutions, at least, have until now been presumed to be above the decay. It was imagined, for example, that they were still reading books in the English faculty at Harvard. But that illusion, too, has been shattered by Professor Sven Birkerts, aged 38, who teaches Creative Writing to undergraduates there. "(**0**) ..*H*.. ," he says in a powerful lament which has just been published by *Harvard Magazine*. Every year, he says, he conducts a survey among his students, and "(**61**) ....." .

The Harvard undergraduates, who have enrolled to study the arts of expository writing under Professor Birkerts are, to put it no higher, reluctant readers.

"The printed page taxes and wearies them.

(**62**) ..... .What hope does a teacher have for getting them to write? Initially, I confess, I always despair. I read through their first papers, so neatly word-processed ... and my heart sinks," he writes, adding: "(**63**) ..... ."

Professor Birkerts said yesterday that the trend away from reading seemed to have reached a critical stage. "(**64**) ..... . It's merely that they are no longer receiving the world through the medium of print," he said. "They find it difficult to sit in front of a stationary page."

Professor Birkerts, who has been teaching at Harvard for five years, wonders in his article how his students imagine they can learn to write without bothering to read. He says that they give all kinds of explanations for their failure to read. "Too busy". "(**65**) .....". "I've always had a hard time with books that are supposed to be good for me". And then, proudly: "If I have time, I like to relax with Stephen King (the popular novelist)."

Professor Birkerts adds: "(**66**) ..... Very likely it will once again be flat."

From The Times

A The writing is almost always flat, monotonous prose

B Most students have video recorders

C It's not lack of interest

D Their handwriting is poor

E Will the world be different if people stop reading?

F the responses are heartbreaking

G I wish I had the time

H Almost none of my students reads independently

I He doesn't think it's a serious problem

J They find little pleasure there

6 *Use the following notes on different stretching exercises from a book about running to prepare fuller instructions. Write* **one complete sentence** *for each numbered set of notes, using connecting words and phrases as appropriate. You may add words or change the form of words given in the notes but do not add any extra information. The first point has been expanded for you as an example.*

Stretching Exercises

Calf stretch

0 Facing wall – so finger tips almost touch it when arms stretched out.

67 Heels firmly on floor – lean forwards, hands resting on wall, so calf muscles slightly stretched.

68 Hold position 30 seconds then lean further – little extra stretch.

Inner thigh

69 Feet wide apart – lean forwards so pushing palms of hands towards floor.

70 Hold 30 seconds – remain relaxed, breathe calmly.

Runner's stretch

71 Left foot forward, right foot back behind you – bend left leg – back straight.

Quadriceps pull

72 Stand right leg – grasp left ankle (left hand), pull up until feel stretch front of thigh.

73 Repeat exercise other leg.

> **Questions 71 and 72:** try to **vary the sentence structure** by beginning *With* ... or with an *-ing* form verb.

Stretching Exercises

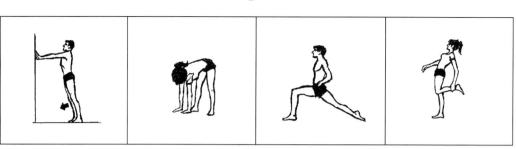

Calf Stretch

0   Stand facing a wall, so that your finger tips can almost reach it when your arms are stretched out.

67

68

Inner thigh

69

70

Runner's stretch

71

Quadriceps pull

72

Study the **example.** Notice the use of the imperative and the way possessive adjectives are used with parts of the body.

Section A

You will hear some information about places to visit in the historic harbour area of the City of Bristol. For questions **1–11,** complete the table by filling in the missing information.

You will hear the recording twice.

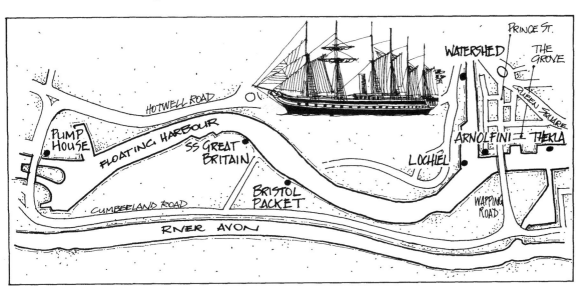

NAME		ORIGINAL USE		CURRENT USE
Watershed	1		2	
Lochiel	3		4	
Arnolfini	5		6	
Thekla		freight steamer	7	
SS Great Britain		first ocean-going iron ship	8	
Pump House	9		10	
Bristol Packet		working narrowboat	11	

Question 2: just give the key information – ignore any extra details.

Question 3: if you're not sure of a word, listen for any extra information which might help to explain it. For example, *letters and packages* may help you to find the answer here.

Questions 9 and 10: be careful! The information isn't given in exactly the same order as the questions.

Section B

Look at the illustrations – they may help you to understand any words you don't know.

▶ *You will hear the details of a recipe. As you listen, you must fill in the information for questions 12–19.*

Listen very carefully as you will hear this piece only ONCE.

If you don't catch the information you need, listen carefully – the world you need may be repeated.

▶

Tomato and Artichoke Salad with Basil

Ingredients

450g [**12**] tomatoes

400g can of artichoke hearts

50g onion

1 large clove of garlic

20ml lemon juice

45ml [**13**]

30ml fromage frais

salt and pepper

fresh basil sprigs

Method

[**14**] the artichoke hearts and cut them in half.

[**15**] the tomatoes. Arrange the artichoke hearts

and tomatoes in a serving dish.

[**16**] the onion. Whisk together the crushed garlic,

lemon juice, oil, fromage frais and seasoning. [**17**]

the onion.

Spoon the dressing over the vegetables and basil.

[**18**] for about 30 minutes.

SERVES 4   NOT SUITABLE [**19**]

88

Section C

*You will hear some advice about interviews. For questions **20–29** complete the sentences with an appropriate word or short phrase.*

You will hear the piece twice.

To ensure that you get selected for interview, it's important to put in a good

20 [   ]

You can either prepare a **21** [   ] curriculum vitae and

a **22** [   ] covering letter or vice versa.

You should prepare for the interview by **23** [   ] about

what you want to say.

If you don't have a clear idea of what you want to get across, the interview will be

24 [   ]

Being able to include key information about yourself, when answering questions

gives you a bit more **25** [   ] the interview.

It's important to use the interviewers' questions as a **26** [   ]

to talk about yourself but try not to appear to be a high **27** [   ]

salesman or saleswoman.

Be aware of **28** [   ] and make sure you're well presented.

If you feel uncomfortable, you probably won't **29** [   ]

in the interview and you're unlikely to get the job.

> Try to predict the answers to **questions 20, 23, and 29.**

> Make sure the word fits grammatically. What verb form follows *by*?.

> Where you hear two possible answers because the speaker has used two words or expressions with the same or similar meaning, you only need to write one of them.

Section D

You will hear five different people talking about difficult interview experiences .
You will hear the recording twice.

Task One

*Letters **A–E** list several different interview results. Decide which one on the list applies in each case. For questions **30–34** put the letter of the result against the appropriate speaker. A letter may need to be used more than once.*

Question 30:
be careful. The information you need here comes at the beginning.

Which speaker describes an interview where the interviewee

▶ **A** was offered the job but didn't take it?

B was offered the job and took it?

C wasn't offered the job?

withdrew: If you don't recognise a word at first, think about it carefully – you may be able to work out the meaning. What happens if you *withdraw* money from a bank?

▶ **D** withdrew from the interview?

E may or may not have been offered the job. We don't know.

SPEAKER 1	30
SPEAKER 2	31
SPEAKER 3	32
SPEAKER 4	33
SPEAKER 5	34

Task Two

*Letters **A–H** list different problems which the interviewees may have had. For questions **35–39** put the letter of the problem against the appropriate interview. Letters may only be used once.*

In which interview was there a problem because the interviewee

A was too relaxed?

B arrived late?

C was upset by the formal atmosphere?

D didn't give a positive enough answer to a question?

E wasn't polite enough?

F didn't like the interviewer's manner?

G wasn't dressed smartly enough?

H hadn't expected to be asked a lot of technical questions?

INTERVIEW 1	35
INTERVIEW 2	36
INTERVIEW 3	37
INTERVIEW 4	38
INTERVIEW 5	39

Work with another student.

Phase A

(about 3 minutes)

- Introduce yourselves to each other.
- Tell your partner about your family. Ask them about theirs.
- Ask your partner what they enjoy watching on television. Explain what your favourite programmes are.
- Tell your partner what your ideal holiday would be. Ask your partner about their ideal holiday.

> Remember to try and introduce some **interesting points** into the conversation.

Phase B

(3 or 4 minutes)

Task 1 (Describe and draw)

Candidate A has a picture to look at. Candidate B has an incomplete version of the same picture. Don't look at each other's pictures.

Candidate A: Turn to the picture on page 141 and describe the scene carefully so that your partner can complete their picture. You have about a minute.

Candidate B: Turn to the picture on page 142 and listen to your partner's description. Fill in any parts which are missing from your picture by drawing the objects (or the shapes of the objects) in the correct places.

> Candidate B – you won't lose marks for putting something in the wrong place.

Now compare the two pictures.

Task 2 (Describe and identify)

Each candidate has four pictures of city scenes. Three of the pictures are the same but in a different order. One of the pictures is different in each case. Don't look at each other's pictures.

Candidate B: Turn to the set of pictures on page 145 and describe them clearly so that your partner can identify them.

Candidate A: Turn to the set of pictures on page 143. Listen to your partner's description and decide which picture is not described. You may make notes if you wish. When B has finished, describe the remaining picture.

> Don't worry if you can't think of the *exact* word for something. You won't lose marks if you find another way to express what you want to say.

> Don't worry if you can't agree completely on an interpretation. Make sure you understand each other's point of view and agree to disagree if necessary.

Phase C

(3 or 4 minutes)

► Look at the photograph on page 141. Talk about it and decide what the photographer was trying to represent.

Do you agree with the photographer's point of view? Why/ Why not?

> You should **both** take part in this report-back stage. Be prepared to ask your partner if you've forgotten anything, or to add any points your partner omits.

Phase D

(3 or 4 minutes)

In this phase the examiner would ask you to report your conclusions about the photograph and then ask a few more questions to continue the discussion.

To practise your reporting skills, work with another pair and take it in turns to summarise and explain the conclusions you reached.

PRACTICE TEST

PAPER 1 READING
1 HOUR 15 MINUTES

Answer **all** questions

How to find out about dinosaurs

Answer questions 1–19 by referring to the review of children's educational books, on page 94.

For questions 1–19 answer by choosing from the sections of the review A–I, on page 94.
*Note: When more than one answer is required, you may give the answers **in any order**.*

Which book or set of books

concerns history?   **1** ....

contains useful lists of facts?   **2** ....   **3** ....

explains scientific terms?   **4** ....

has been published for many years?   **5** ....

contains well-known sayings?   **6** ....

has an introduction explaining how to use the book?   **7** ....

In which book or set of books could you find

maps   **8** ....   **9** ....

lots of close-up photographs   **10** ....

cartoon-style drawings   **11** ....

sections which you can lift up or pull out?   **12** ....

Which book or set of books does the author think

would be suitable for children under 10 years old?   **13** ....

would also be suitable for adults?   **14** ....   **15** ....

looks rather old-fashioned?   **16** ....

is very good value for money?   **17** ....

has photographs which are rather ridiculous?   **18** ....

is the best produced and most complete?   **19** ....

How to find out about dinosaurs

A When buying an encyclopedia, you will find that the basic choice lies between fat single volumes, with useful but necessarily limited entries, and larger and costlier multi-volume sets. It is possible to purchase single volumes by subject area, which build up to form a comprehensive reference library, but none that I have seen compares for authority, design and breadth with the new **Oxford Children's Encyclopedia** (OUP £100). I cannot fault it. It is beautifully clear and has been laid out intelligently and attractively. Information is easy to find and children will gain confidence through learning how to cross-refer, and in the process will hit upon innumerable interesting side-shoots of information.

The encyclopedia uses a variety of illustrative styles: line drawings, cross-sections, maps, charts, diagrams and excellent photographs with good clear reproduction in sharp focus. Explanations are lucid, but there is some depth to them. Each entry gives basic information and has a See-Also box, to guide the reader further.

Every home with children would do well to buy a set and it is not to be despised by adults for their own use, either.

B The **Dorling Kindersley Children's Illustrated Encyclopedia** (£25) has the unmistakable design trademark of that firm – much use of large, close-up photographs of objects, clear typeface, good quality paper. It is divided into topics rather than arranged alphabetically. If you need to know about, say cork, you consult the index, and are referred to the section on trees, in which you will find your relevant paragraph. Once children have read the How to Use This Book pages at the beginning, they should have no problem in finding their way around. Whereas the Oxford set will suit children best as the progress towards their GCSE years, the Dorling Kindersley encyclopedia is a particularly good choice for the under-10s.

C Kingfisher score high marks for their **Science Encyclopedia** (£25), which has no rival and fills a serious gap in the market brilliantly. Each entry has a symbol beside it, referring to a key at the front of the book, which indicates what general division of science it relates to – astronomy, physics, life sciences and so on. There does not appear to be a scientific term, discovery, principle or personality that does not have an entry. The entries are clear, interesting, well-illustrated and convey the real excitement of studying science.

D That good old standby, **The Junior Pears Encyclopedia**, now in its 31st year and edited by Edward Blishen (Pelham £10.99), is a book to have handy by the homework desk for checking facts or giving brief explanations, it also contains those lists so beloved of a certain type of small boy: a Diary of World Events, The Highest Mountains in the World, Historic Acts of Parliament, Manned Spacecraft launched up to December 1990.

E Some of the non-fiction series now look dated and dreary, set against so much that is attractive and fresh. I wouldn't, for example, spend money on a series such as the **On the Map** (Simon and Schuster £4.99 each), one-volume introductions to countries of the world. Nothing new is attempted, with dull slabs of minimal text plonked beside uninterestingly arranged picture-library photographs of the usual French market, Eiffel Tower, Paris traffic variety. Altogether, it's a little too like a 1960s textbook to attract those buying books for home use.

F Geography is not easy to get right, but few inquisitive children could resist **The Picture Atlas of the World** (Dorling Kindersley £9.99). This is an absolute bargain, arranged alphabetically, with a two-page spread per country, beautiful maps, dotted with information in relief, and bordered by a section of Facts and Figures, a general paragraph of introduction, and some particularly important points highlighted in their own box. It brings the world alive.

G In a desperate effort to stave off children's boredom with historical topics, the **I Was There series** (Bodley head £7.99 each volume) uses photographs of actors and extras dressed up and posing as Vikings battling, ancient Egyptians eating and writing on papyrus, medieval knights donning armour piece by piece. They look extremely unconvincing and rather silly.

H As a first thesaurus for children aged six and over, **The Kingfisher Book of Words** by George Beal (£7.99) is endlessly useful. Quotations, idioms and proverbs are cogently presented, well laid out and the whole book is cheered by cartoon-style line-drawings, illustrating for example, crocodile tears.

I Finally, I can recommend the perfect present for motor-mad infants – **Car** by Angela Royston and Colin King (Frances Lincoln £8.99). How a car works and how it can be mended are demonstrated and explained by flaps that can be lifted and tabs that can be pulled. Like all the best non-fiction for children, it is equally accessible to ignorant adults.

From The Sunday Times

Second text/questions 20–25

*For questions **20–25** you must choose which of the paragraphs **A–G** match the numbered gaps in the newspaper article. There is one extra paragraph which does not belong in any of the gaps.*

Science Report

Healthier way of life underground

By Martin Knights

A remote area of north-west China is the home for a unique group of people who are known as the cave-dwellers of Shanxi. They have been the subject of an extensive study which shows that their underground life-style is apparently healthier than those of urban and rural communities more exposed to the elements.

20

Respiratory complaints such as asthma and bronchitis have been cured and rheumatism and skin conditions vastly improved as a result of prolonged periods of habitation underground.

Research on the cave dwellers started 50 years ago, and at a recent symposium in Beijing statistical evidence assembled over that period was quoted to support several startling observations.

The people of Shanxi seem to have chosen an underground home that possesses the optimum environment in terms of stability of temperature and relative humidity.

21

The best conditions exist when the temperature is in the range of 10°C to 22°C and the relative humidity is between 30 and 75 per cent. The atmosphere of the Shanxi cave dwellings is within those ranges.

22

Colds were only experienced among those who regu-

larly went in and out of the caves. There was a lower incidence of rhumatism. Skin problems were rare.

The scientists maintain that stress and irrational effects caused by noise were infrequent. An additional explanation for longevity and excellent health was lower exposure to radioactive substances in the atmosphere.

Another observation was that hens were more productive, laying a greater number of, and bigger eggs all year round.

23

Patients suffering from asthma, bronchitis, insomnia or nervous disorders are treated in special reception areas located at 1,000 ft below surface for up to two weeks. The quiet stable environment is conducive to the curing of these disorders.

24

The two million or so asthmatics in the UK would certainly enjoy the benefits that controlled therapy in an underground environment would bring to their lives.

25

The ultimate cure for many asthmatics is the building up of resistance to attacks in an environment where harmful atmospheric effects are reduced. Maybe the "cave therapy" could open up a new life for caves in Britain.

A In particular, the dust-free clean air of the underground dwellings has produced a cure rate on adult and child bronchitis and asthma sufferers of 84 per cent and 96 per cent respectively.

B The temperature of the ground is nearly constant between 30 and 100 ft below surface. Above or below this margin the temperature is affected either by seasonal changes or will increase as one approaches the Earth's centre.

C Drugs that ease and control the respiratory function of asthmatics only alleviate the discomfort temporarily.

D They suffer less disease and their longevity has recently been cited as a benefit of living underground.

E The findings lend support to recent studies in the Soviet Union into a form of "cave therapy" that has been practised since the late sixties.

F Scientists are unable to offer any explanation for these surprising results as yet, but further studies are planned in the future.

G Research attributes many benefits to those conditions: reduced incidence of diseases and reduced infection to the ear, nose and throat.

Third text/questions 26–31

Read the newspaper article below and then answer the questions on page **97.**

Curing the ill-mannered

Amateur actress Margeret Davies knows what it is to suffer for her art: over the past few years she has played characters with arthritis, severe depression, thyroid disturbances, and mysterious dizzy spells.

Davies is a simulated patient, her roles based on real case histories but replayed as authentically as possible to medical students as part of their course in communication skills.

The project at Leicester University is in the vanguard of a campaign to put such skills at the centre of medicine rather than at its periphery. As senior lecturer Brian McAvoy explains, "Good communication is not just the icing on the cake. It's an essential part of being a competent physician."

Doctors' failings in this area are legendary. It is a rare patient who has never encountered at least one example of impatience, indifference, abruptness, tactlessness, insensitivity or just downright rudeness. All too often bedside manners are indistinguishable from bad manners.

Dr David Pendleton, editor of the book *Doctor-Patient Communication*, says the problem starts, with the selection of students, when a certain kind of academic prowess is emphasized to the exclusion of other vital qualities. Training makes matters worse: "If something can't be medicalized it's not thought to be the doctor's province, so normal communication gets lost.

We then overwork them so badly it's hard for them to retain what last scrap of humanity they might have."

Pendleton would like to see a selection process that taps into motivation, for example, without forfeiting academic excellence, plus more

career guidance within the profession so that those who are neither interested in nor good with people could be directed towards the laboratory rather than the surgery.

Doctors are well aware of the communication problem. For his doctorate Pendleton carried out a study in the Oxford region and found that the doctors thought there was a barrier in about a quarter of their consultations. Key factors included the patient being a lot younger than the doctor, the patient being very tense, confused or shy and the patient being of a lower social class. The sex of either party did not seem to matter, nor did the length of the doctor's experience.

In McAvoy's sessions a student's tutor and peers can comment on his approach and the "patient" can step out of role and join the discussion.

Davies and her fellow actors are briefed in the character's personality as well as medical history. In this way students can encounter aggression, reticence and garrulousness. Sessions are replayed on video later. McAvoy believes the feedback from a simulated patient is invaluable. "Real patients may be afraid or embarrassed to say, for instance, that the spontaneous hand on the shoulder was very much appreciated or that they disliked the way the doctor wouldn't look them in the eye."

His course in the Department of General Practice is rare in being compulsory. Many schools make communication an optional extra if they offer it at all.

There is, however, growing awareness of its importance. The UK Network for Communication in Health Care was founded recently by inter-

ested professionals, to push for more and better teaching at every level.

Penny Morris is the network's convenor and a research and teaching fellow in communication skills at Cambridge University attached to Addenbrooke's Hospital. "Of course there are those who believe that though this sort of thing is important it can't actually be taught. But on the whole there is now an enormous amount of goodwill among doctors to learn."

"People are not fooled by a smooth manner. They don't want to be reassured and fobbed off, they want information. Good communication is not just about being nice and charming, because you can have bags of charm and still be a disaster. Nor is it about teaching doctors manipulation skills. Simple things such as courtesy and patience are important because they are about valuing people. They imply a basic respect. And we like to stress that doctors who do these things have a better time, the difficulties are more bearable, the job more enjoyable."

From The Times

26 Margaret Davies is able to help with the project at Leicester University because

    A   she trained as a medical student.

    B   she has had personal experience of several illnesses.

    C   she is a skilled teacher.

    D   she can play the role of a patient realistically.

27 Examples of doctors' poor communication skills

    A   are greatly exaggerated.

    B   are widely known.

    C   are the subject of many jokes.

    D   are rarely encountered.

28 Dr Pendleton believes that the situation could be improved by

    A   raising the academic standards of medical courses.

    B   attracting more people to join the medical profession.

    C   improving the process of selecting medical students.

    D   making medical students work in laboratories more.

29 Research has shown that doctors find difficulty in communicating with patients when

    A   the doctor is extremely tired.

    B   the doctor is relatively inexperienced.

    C   there is a big age gap between doctor and patient.

    D   the patient is in pain.

30 Actors are particularly useful in the training sessions because they

    A   are able to discuss their reactions to a doctor's approach openly.

    B   can replay the same consultations more than once.

    C   are not embarrassed about discussing their medical symptoms.

    D   can show stronger emotions than real patients.

31 According to Penny Morris, improved communication skills can lead to

    A   more patients attending doctors surgeries.

    B   increased job satisfaction for doctors.

    C   a higher success rate in treating disease.

    D   greater respect for doctors from the public.

Fourth text/questions 32–49

*Answer questions **32–49** by referring to the newspaper article on page **99**. Choose your answers from the travel agents **A–G,** which are mentioned in the article.*

*Note: When a question requires more than one answer, you may give the answers **in any order.***
Some choices may be required more than once.

In which travel agencies were the following holiday destinations recommended ?

Malta	**32**	
Turkey	**33**	**34** ....
Italy (Sorrento)	**35**	**36** ....
Spain (Ibiza/Menorca)	**37**	
Cyprus	**38**	
Greece (Rhodes)	**39**	
North Africa (Tunisia/Morocco)	**40**	

In which travel agents did the travel consultant

have personal experience of a place which they recommended?	**41**	**42**	**43** ....
check flight availability from airports in cities other than London?	**44**	**45**	
know about, or give full details of, the company's insurance policy?	**46**	**47**	
ignore the customer until he asked for help?	**48**		
advise the customer to use public transport rather than hire a car?	**49**		

Looking for the special agents

Most people turn to their high street travel agent when they decide to book a package holiday. But how do you know which ones will provide the personal service you want and suggest options to fit your criteria? EDWARD WELSH sought help at 12 branches, some of which came up with answers.

To test the leading travel agency chains, I visited a branch of each in mid-January – at the height of the traditional holiday booking season – and sought help in selecting a package for four people: myself, my wife – we are both in our twenties – and her middle-aged parents.

I outlined our requirements as follows:

- A two-week Mediterranean holiday in July, staying in a four-star hotel with half-board at a cost of up to £500 each. The accommodation should be by the sea but in a spot that was not too noisy or crowded and was close to interesting places to visit.

My other questions were:

- Could car hire be arranged?
- Could my wife's parents fly out from a different airport?
- Would it be possible to have full details of the agency's holiday insurance policy, listing all the contingencies excluded from the cover?

travel agent A

Margaret did not take long to work out what kind of holiday would suit my group. Ignoring all the brochures on show, she disappeared for a few minutes to find a selection of literature and began working out in which resorts we could afford to stay. This narrowed our choice to North Africa and Italy.

She felt Tunisia and Morocco would be excellent for beaches – and there would be some excursions to archeological remains and bazaars – but her real enthusiasm was for Italy. After tirelessly searching for somewhere within our price range we settled on Sorrento, a town she herself had visited. Her view was that there were excellent places to visit from Sorrento and, although the beaches were not fantastic, it was possible to swim in the sea. The two hotels Margaret suggested were within our budget, but – and this she failed to point out – only as long as we didn't opt for a sea view.

Nonetheless, I was impressed by her knowledge and confidence and by the fact that she was conversant with her agency's travel insurance policy and could provide me with its details in full.

travel agent B

It's rare to find a well-travelled agent, but Mary had been to Rhodes and so could tell me about the noisy town of Lindos; and she warned against hiring a car from just any company in Greece. Nonetheless, some of her suggestions were rather suspect.

On Rhodes, Mary's suggestion was affordable but too isolated even for the older, peace-seeking members of my party.

Her personal experience came to the fore, though, when she suggested Sorrento. She had stayed in the hotel she suggested, and knew that the lack of beach was compensated for by the hotel's private swimming jetties.

Whenever she found a good hotel she worked hard to find a better alternative and used the company's hotel guide extensively. Mary was keen to help and confident of her own knowledge, I left with a wide selection of holiday options which showed some attempt on her part to come up with something different and, in one case for me at least, appealing.

travel agent C

Although the agency was relatively busy, Nicole was happy to devote some time to helping me. Twice she went into a back office to dig up the brochures of smaller, more specialist tour operators whose literature was not displayed in the front office. And she was full of ideas for places to holiday.

But, despite the hard work, she appeared to know little about the holidays she was trying to sell. Her suggested destinations included noisy, crowded Greek islands, such as Kos or Mykonos, or equally unsuitable parts of Turkey. She did not make me aware that flights to some of these Greek destinations only leave mid-week – an important detail for someone who can only take weekend to weekend holidays. From the brochures she was recommending, she was unable to find a four-star hotel that was within our budget, although at least one such does exist. She therefore began putting forward the idea of staying in apartments or villas, or going instead to the Menorca or Ibiza.

Nicole knew nothing about the insurance policies on offer: she was either new to the job or lacked confidence in her own judgement. In terms of seeking useful information, I was wasting my time.

travel agent D

With only two counter staff and dozens of people pouring in every hour I was amazed that Lynn spent one hour and 10 minutes trying to help me find the right kind of holiday. But, despite her conscientious work, her advice only directed me to two of Turkey's more over-run resorts.

Working from the Go Turkey brochure, Lynn pointed out the fact that the prices listed did not include flight supplements and she suggested we forget car hire because public transport was so reliable and cheap – good advice. For any information she did not know, she contacted the tour operator. But most importantly, Lynn checked the availability of flights from Manchester and Gatwick and hotels I had selected. This was useful because one of my selections was fully booked at the time I was supposed to stay there.

In the end, we found that there was space at a suitable hotel near Bodrum in a relatively isolated spot near this still-attractive, yet busy town. The other option was a "B" class hotel close to the centre of Kusadasi, a noisy, tourist-orientated town but with first-class access to the incredible classical sites in the region. Of the hotel, the brochure itself warns: "some noise is possible from a nearby bar/restaurant'.

A pity, I thought, that Lynn had spent so long helping me with such uninspiring results.

travel agent E

Judith put a lot of effort into helping – tirelessly checking availability and prices – but few of her suggestions passed the "I'd be tempted" test.

Her first idea was Majorca which she had visited herself, but the two hotels she suggested – although in a sandy bay away from the island's largest resort – were modern high-rise blocks.

Judith came up with many other recommendations such as the Costa del Sol, Cyprus and Crete, warning me off their noisier areas.

She handed me a useful leaflet listing car hire services throughout the Mediterranean and a copy of the agency's travel insurance which listed details in full.

Judith's hard work has to be commended but she was directing me towards the more expensive resorts or hotels in a mass-market areas in the Mediterranean.

travel agent F

With the shop stuffed with travel consultants, you would have thought that a customer might receive some useful, personalised advice. But in fact this was supermarket holiday shopping of the highest order.

I was ignored until I asked for advice and, despite Liz's attachment to her computerised booking screen, she was unable to hide the glazed look of indifference on her face. She desultorily picked up Intasun's 260-page brochure and recommended the Algarve.

She checked flight availability from Manchester and Birmingham and worked out the total costs per person including all supplements. But, despite the computer wizardry, Liz was unable to find many affordable options. She suggested a three-star or a four-star hotel in the centre of Faro away from the beach and – when I asked about other resorts – she came up with Malta and Lanzarote. She added that it was up to me to decide because there are "millions" of places to holiday and she did not really know what kind of package I was looking for. This came as no surprise at all.

From *The Sunday Times*

Instructions to candidates

*This paper contains one Section A task and four Section B tasks. You must complete the Section A task and **one** task from Section B.*

The two sections carry equal marks.

*Read the instructions and consider the information **carefully** both for section A and the task you select for Section B.*

Section A

1   You are going to attend a one-month English language course in Britain and have asked to stay with a local family during that time. You have just received two letters, one from the language school and one from the family, and it is clear to you that the accommodation which has been arranged is not suitable. Read the school advertisement, the extracts from the letters and the handwritten notes you have made on them carefully and then, **using the information given**, write the two letters listed on page 101.

I am writing to tell you that I have arranged family accommodation for you from 2nd to 28th March, as you requested. You will be staying with Mr and Mrs Hall at the following address:

"Lake View"
Nine Tree Hill
Churchill
BS14 3TZ

I said £70 max

I said I'd be arriving on 1st.

The cost for this accommodation is £75 per week, which includes bed, breakfast and evening meal, and this sum should be paid to Mrs Hall direct.

Mrs Hall will be writing to you separately and I would be grateful if you could contact her as soon as possible to confirm these arrangements and to give her details of your arrival time.

Please do not hesitate to write to me if you have any further queries.

Yours sincerely,

Jane Woolworth

Jane Woolworth (Accommodation Officer)

The Sundown School of English

Learn English in the lovely south west

- small classes
- highly-qualified staff
- individual attention
- General English, Business English
- accommodation with carefully-selected local families

13 Porringer Road, Oxmouth, OE2 5XY

We are delighted to hear that you are coming to stay with us and we look forward very much to meeting you when you arrive on 2nd March.

In the meantime, I thought we'd tell you something about ourselves. We have three lively children, Emma (4), Tom (7) and Harry (14) as well as four cats, three rabbits and a dog! We hope you like music – Tom has just started learning the violin while Harry plays the electric guitar and his dearest wish is to play in a rock band!

The children can't wait for you to arrive – I'm sure you'll love them. We are hoping you'll be willing to do some baby-sitting for us while you're here, as my husband and I like to go out two or three nights a week.

We live in a lovely old house, about 10 minutes' walk from the village of Churchill. Buses go into town every two hours and the journey takes about 40 minutes. You'll have to take another bus from the centre in order to get to the school – I'll check on the details before you arrive.

The school said you wouldn't mind sharing a room with another student and we're now waiting to find out who your room-mate will be.

We hope to hear from you soon,

Brenda Hall

Brenda Hall (Mrs)

[handwritten note:] I asked for somewhere quiet!

[handwritten note:] What a nerve!

[handwritten note:] out of the question – I stipulated a single room

[handwritten note:] Hardly local! much too inconvenient

Now write

(a) **a** brief **letter** to Mrs Hall explaining that you will not be coming to stay with her (write about 50 words).

(b) **a letter** to the school pointing out the problems with the accommodation and asking for alternative arrangements to be made (write about 200 words).

Choose ONE of the following writing tasks. Your answer should follow exactly the instructions given. Write approximately 250 words.

2   This announcement has appeared in a local English language magazine.

Be a radio star!

"English Alive", your local English language radio station, has been on the air for one year. Up till now, our programming has been limited to two hours a day of mainly news and information. As from January 1st, however, our airtime is to be doubled and, to celebrate, we are holding a competition to find the best suggestions for new programmes for the coming year. The winner will appear as a guest presenter on "English Alive".

To enter the competition and have the chance of becoming a radio star send a proposal for new programmes. Include **clear** details of the programmes you suggest and explain **why** you think they would be of interest to "English Alive" listeners.

Write your entry for the competition.

3   You have been asked by a college magazine to write **an article** aimed at new students, entitled *Studying Successfully: A Beginner's Guide.*

Write a light-hearted but helpful article. You should describe the facilities available and mention a range of good study habits, recommending the ones which you have personally found most helpful.

4   This is part of a letter you receive from a friend.

As I told you, I've been seriously thinking of taking a year off before I go to university and my parents seem to think it would be a good thing too. What do you think of the idea of spending the time in your country? I've only been on short visits before but I'd really like to get to know the country better and it would be great if I was living some-where near you so I could visit you and your family. The big question is: What should I do in the time? Attend a course? Be an au pair? Do voluntary work? I'd like to be near other students and I'd also need somewhere to stay that's not too expensive Have you got any ideas?

Write to your friend giving **practical suggestions**, referring to the points in the letter.

5   An English friend is doing a project on "green" issues round the world and has written to ask you about attitudes towards nature conservation and the recycling of waste materials in your country.

Write **a report** which you can send to him/her.

Answer **all** questions.

Section A

1 *For questions 1–15, read the article below and circle the letter next to the word which best fits each space. The exercise begins with an example (0).*

Hotels pick up bills for five-star thieves

For the latest edition of *AA Hotels and Restaurants in Britain and Ireland* the AA (0) ....questioned....

2,000 hotels about the way their guests behave. The survey proves, the AA says, that the

(1) .... the hotel's star rating, the greater its bill for thieving guests. Brian Sack, partner

of the Sharrow Bay Country House Hotel on Ullswater, noticing a guest with three ashtrays in her

handbag, deftly (2) .... two of them with the gentle reproof that one should be enough.

Thefts (3) .... from the petty: TV remote control batteries, light (4) ....,

room numbers and fire assembly (5) ...., through the curious: a single strip of

wallpaper and a picture of Miss World 1988, to the major: grandfather clocks, a grand piano,

two beds, a stuffed bear, a dance floor carpet and a complete (6) .... of onions taken

from the garden of the Longueville Manor hotel in Jersey.

Things guests (7) .... behind included false teeth, glass eyes, wigs, a sack of snakes

and a box of poisonous spiders.

Some hotels suffered quite serious (8) .... One had its front door kicked down by

three soldiers who had been (9) .... out. At the Seckford Hall Hotel in Suffolk, a

sleepwalking guest wrenched a radiator off the wall, (10) .... rooms. One manager

(11) .... "my nose" under items which had been broken.

Room service (12) .... included jam sandwiches and fillet steak for a dog; fried eggs

and ice cream and chocolate sauce.

Hoteliers said that some guests' complaints were ridiculous. Bad weather (13) ....

offence, though other natural phenomena that (14) .... guests included birdsong and the

sound of the sea. One guest at the Seacrest Hotel in Hampshire, complained to the tourist board

about a hurricane that had (15) .... him awake. The roof of the hotel had blown off.

From The Times

103

0	A examined	B checked	C questioned	D reviewed
1	A bigger	B higher	C more expensive	D more famous
2	A withdrew	B pulled	C stole	D removed
3	A range	B spread	C reach	D cover
4	A bulbs	B bells	C balls	D tubes
5	A advertisements	B notes	C notices	D signals
6	A bunch	B crop	C bundle	D flock
7	A let	B forget	C leave	D lose
8	A damages	B breakages	C injury	D destruction
9	A closed	B stuck	C barred	D locked
10	A flooding	B overflowing	C spilling	D draining
11	A named	B explained	C marked	D listed
12	A commands	B bills	C requests	D claims
13	A made	B caused	C produced	D did
14	A upset	B resented	C embarrassed	D hurt
15	A held	B brought	C made	D kept

2 For questions **16–30**, complete the following article by writing the missing words in the spaces provided. **Use only one word in each space.** The exercise begins with an example **(0)**.

Forest Fires

The Gagadju aborigines of northern Australia warn **(0)** ....*every*.... generation of their people

not to burn the rainforest, **(16)**.............. they live. **(17)** .... who sets fire **(18)** ....

the trees, they say, may be struck blind by the spirits of the forest blowing back **(19)** ....

his face. **(20)** .... much of the forest is now **(21)** .... burnt that great bands of

fire, spreading across much of the tropics **(22)** .... easily be seen from space. And, it

(23) .... , we *are* being afflicted by a kind of blindness. **(24)** .... the forest burns,

a million species may soon become extinct. Water sources on which a billion people depend

(25) .... food are likely to dry **(26)** .... The land will turn **(27)** .... desert.

And the world's climate itself will change. **(28)** .... all this destruction is often merely to

provide packaging for consumer products, or to raise cattle for the American fast food trade.

Much serves short-term political ends. It is as **(29)** .... the smoke, blowing back from the

forest, were fatally shortening **(30)** .... sight.

Adapted from an article in *Paradise Lost*, published by Earthlife, in association with the Observer.

3 In **most** lines of the following text, there is **one** mistake with a verb. It is either the wrong tense or the wrong form in some other way. For each numbered line **31–45**, underline the incorrect verb and then write the correct form of the verb in the space provided. Some lines are correct. Indicate these lines with a tick (√). The exercise begins with two examples **(0)**.

Flu Takes Area by Storm

The flu, that unwelcome wintertime visitor, descends with

particular vengeance on much of the Washington area this season,

according to doctors and public health officials across the region.

"We are being killed with the flu," said Peg Mastal, chief nurse in

the Kaiser Health Care Programme, a large health maintenance

organization. "Our phone lines are jammed the day after

Christmas," said Mastal, adding that some of the doctors

had given up part of their holiday to help dealing with the demand.

For many sufferers, this is being a season of problems. The

weekend before Christmas, Jennette Vernon, of Wheaton, had to

finish buy gifts, prepare a holiday dinner for 10 and organize

birthday parties for all three of her young children. She also

had a sore throat, a temperature of 39° C and aches spreading

through her limbs. "I was tried to put on a good act for the kids,

so they won't feel that Mommy didn't want to be with them at

Christmas," said Vernon, "but I thought, "I want to crawl into my

bed, pull the covers over my head and just had some sleep.'"

"This is the worst I had seen it in a while," said Frank Palumbo, a

district pediatrician. He said that the families of some of his

patients cancelling holiday trips, adding that the flu is not much

fun for doctors to treat, "You don't make people feeling better

right away." He, like most doctors, recommend bed rest, plenty

of fluids and painkillers.

0	has descended
0	√
31	....
32	....
33	....
34	....
35	....
36	....
37	....
38	....
39	....
40	....
41	....
42	....
43	....
44	....
45	....

From *The Washington Post*

4 For questions **46–58,** read the following formal advertisement for a job in a restaurant and use the information in it to complete the numbered gaps in the informal advertisement. **Use no more than two words** for each gap. The exercise begins with an example **(0)**. The words you need **do not occur** in the formal advertisement.

Formal advertisement

Part-time restaurant staff (16 – 24) required.
Must be sociable, energetic, and able to work under pressure.
Duties: waiting at table, washing-up, occasional help with preparing food
7.30 – 11.30, Saturday and/or Sunday.
Pay: £10 per day + tips.
Interviews can be arranged by telephoning the following number.

Bloxham 376152

Informal advertisement

Are you (0) ....*aged between*.... **16 and 24?**

Have you got a few hours to (46) .... **at (47)** .... **?**

Do you enjoy (48) .... **people?**

Would you like to (49) .... **some extra cash?**

If the answer to these questions is "yes", read on ...

We are **(50)** .... young people to help in our busy restaurant. You will be working in

a friendly, informal atmosphere, taking customers' orders and serving food, washing the

(51) .... and even lending **(52)** .... with the cooking

(53) .... to time! Things get pretty hectic sometimes, so you'll need to be able to

keep a cool **(54)** ....

There are two **(55)** .... shifts on Saturdays and Sundays and you can work

(56) .... suits you best (or both if you like). The pay is £10 per shift but remember that

(57) .... you get on top of the basic wage are yours to keep!

Interested? Call the number **(58)** .... as soon as possible to arrange an interview.

We look forward to hearing from you!

Bloxham 376152

---

5 *For questions **59–66**, read through the following text and then choose from the list **A–L** the best phrase or sentence given below to fill each of the blanks. Write one letter (**A–L**) in each space. **Some of the suggested answers do not fit at all.** One answer has been given as an example.*

Health Advice for Travellers

Doctors tend to be poor educators; we have depressingly little to show for our efforts to educate the general public on even such a clear-cut issue as the effects of cigarette smoking on health. (**0**) ...K... is it for doctors to provide large numbers of departing travellers with detailed information and effective advice for their trip when the usual forum for doing so is a single, hurried consultation, just before departure. There are limits to what can be achieved in or should be expected from a medical consultation (**59**) .... , even when the doctor is well-motivated and well-informed about the subject, and the traveller is receptive, has a perfect memory, and is good at doing what he or she is told.

What kind of advice should travellers receive? A list of rules and instructions (**60**) .... carries the implication that travellers are incapable of understanding the principles involved, are not interested, or do not 'need' to know. (**61**) .... advice offered on such condescending terms is seldom followed for long. The best advice is not a list of do's and don'ts, (**62**) .... , a clear, rational explanation from which a conclusion is obvious. (**63**) .... and I believe that travellers should have the opportunity to choose for themselves how much they 'want' or 'need' to know.

(**64**) .... , we have studiously avoided giving advice to consult a doctor without stating the reason for doing so. "Consult your doctor" is a useful formula to enable advice-givers to avoid difficult issues, but is a particularly unhelpful one when it relates to a problem which may arise abroad. (**65**) .... to find a doctor in a remote place. Merely finding a doctor does not guarantee that the correct advice or treatment will be given. Some 85% of the world's population have never seen a doctor, and never will. Advice for travellers must take account of the fact that travellers to many parts of the world will be (**66**) ....

From *Traveller's Health*

A Information is a powerful weapon,	**G** in the same position
B It is hardly surprising that	**H** given without explanation or justifications
C But despite this	**I** It is not easy
D Throughout this book	**J** based on the principle
E but is based on information	**K** How much more difficult, then
F It is essential	**L** under the best of circumstances

107

6 *Use the following notes to write about the Irish writer, James Joyce. Write **one complete sentence** for each numbered set of notes, using connecting words and phrases as appropriate. You may add words or change the form of words given in the notes but do not add any extra information. The first point has been expanded for you as an example.*

James Joyce (1882 – 1941)

0 Born Dublin - although wrote almost exclusively about city, spent most adult life abroad (chiefly France).

67 Educated Belvedere College - later university in Dublin – studied philosophy and languages and took interest in theatre.

68 Left Ireland 1904 already convinced destiny as great writer – went first Zurich then Trieste (earned living teaching English).

69 By 1904 completed collection short stories *Dubliners* – problems with publisher prevented publication 10 years.

70 First novel *A Portrait of the Artist as a Young Man* (1916) immediately recognised as masterpiece – many enthusiastic reviews.

71 1922 most famous novel *Ulysses* – written over seven years – very detailed description of day in lives of various Dubliners – published France.

72 Remained Paris after 1920 – poor eyesight – necessary use friends as readers and secretaries – completed last work *Finnegan's Wake* two years before death (1941).

James Joyce (1882 - 1941)

0 James Joyce was born in Dublin and, although he went on to write almost exclusively about that city, he spent most of his adult life abroad, chiefly in France.

67

68

69

70

71

72

Section A

You will hear some advice about preventing car crime. For questions **1–10**, *complete the table by filling in the missing information.*

You will hear the recording twice.

Keep Your Car Secure

Having your car stolen leads to delay and | **1** _____ | .

Remember that car crime is the most | **2** _____ | of all crimes.

Luggage and valuables

Don't leave them | **3** _____ | . Never

leave | **4** _____ | in the glove compartment.

Doors

Lock them every time you leave your car.

Windows

Have | **5** _____ | number etched

on all glassware.

C118 ADF

Ignition Key

Remove the ignition key even when your car is

| **6** _____ |

Aerials

Put your aerial down when you park.

Cassettes/radios

Choose a security-coded model or one which

can be **7** [   ] .

Wheels

Fit lockable wheel nuts to protect wheels.

Fuel cap

A lockable fuel cap forces thieves to

8 [   ] your car when it runs out of petrol.

Documents

Never leave vehicle documents in the car.

They could help a thief to **9** [   ] .

Parking

Park in a busy **10** [   ] area.

Section B

You will hear about a number of auction sales on a telephone information service. As you listen, you must fill in the information for questions 11–17.

Listen very carefully as you will hear this piece only ONCE.

Auction Calendar

Billingsgate Office: 23 Flounder Way, London S14 0ZT

Opening Hours: Monday - Friday: 9.00 am - 5.30 pm

Sunday: | **11** |

*   *   *

March

2nd   Old Master Paintings

3rd | **12** |

4th   Books, Atlases and Maps

8th | **13** |

10th   Rock and Pop Memorabilia

16th | **14** |

19th   Classic Cars

25th | **15** |

*   *   *

Sales are on view for | **16** | before the auction date.

| **17** | can be ordered by telephone (071 543 2021)

Section C

*You wil hear part of a radio interview with a doctor on the subject of jet lag. For questions **18–28**, complete the sentences with an appropriate word or short phrase.*

You will hear the piece twice.

The dictionary describes jet lag as a slight sense of **18** [   ]

and **19** [   ] which is experienced after a long journey by air

The doctor explains that we all have body rhythms which are affected by clock

time, **20** [   ] , and by whether it's day or night.

The symptoms of jet lag include problems with **21** [   ]

and eating, and also with one's mental and physical **22** [   ]

Recovering from jet lag generally takes about one day for each

23 [   ] that you've crossed.

Your recovery rate can be affected by the **24** [   ] and

even the culture of the country you're going to.

You can buy anti-jet lag products but there's **25** [   ]

that they are effective.

To avoid jet lag, the doctor suggests trying to **26** [   ]

on the aeroplane and advises against **27** [   ] meals.

He also recommends avoiding important appointments for

28 [   ] after arrival.

112

Section D

You will hear four different people talking about ways of avoiding jet lag when travelling long distance.

You will hear the recording twice.

Task One

*Letters **A–D** list the subjects the different speakers mention. As you listen, complete the boxes **29–32** with the appropriate letter **A–D**. You may use a letter more than once.*

Who talks

A only about sleeping?

B only about sleeping and drinking?

C only about sleeping and eating?

D about sleeping, eating and drinking?

SPEAKER 1	29
SPEAKER 2	30
SPEAKER 3	31
SPEAKER 4	32

Task Two

*Letters **E–I** list other points the speakers mention. As you listen, complete the boxes **33–37** with the appropriate letter **E–I**. You may use a letter more than once.*

Who mentions that

E there are times when they feel very sleepy?

F they sometimes sleep for 24 hours?

G they suffer from jet lag more on some journeys than others?

H they try to adapt to local time?

I they don't try to adapt to local time?

SPEAKER 1	33		
SPEAKER 2	34		
SPEAKER 3	35		
SPEAKER 4	36	37	

Work in groups of three. One student should play the role of the examiner, giving instructions, asking further questions and making sure both candidates play an equal part in the conversation.

Phase A

(about 3 minutes)

- The examiner and candidates introduce themselves.
- Tell the examiner a little bit about your partner.
- Ask your partner about a book you've really enjoyed reading. Ask your partner to tell you about the kind of reading they enjoy.
- Tell your partner about a sport you play or like to watch. Find out what sports your partner enjoys, if any.

Phase B

(3 or 4 minutes)

Task 1 (Describe and identify)

Candidate A has eight pictures of houses. Candidate B has the same pictures but in a different order. Don't look at each other's pictures.

Candidate A: Turn to the set of pictures on page 146 and describe **two** of them clearly so that your partner can identify them.

Candidate B: Turn to the set of pictures on page 145. Listen to your partner's description and decide which pictures are being described. You may make notes if you wish. At the end, if you still need help, you can ask your partner one or two questions. What helped you identify the pictures?

Task 2 (Describe and relate)

You will each have a picture to look at. The pictures are different but they have a common theme. Don't look at each other's pictures.

Candidate B: Turn to the picture on page 146 and describe what you can see. You have about a minute.

Candidate A: Turn to the picture on page 144 and listen to your partner's description. You can make notes on a piece of paper if you wish. When B has finished, say what you think the common theme is.

Now compare the two pictures.

Phase C

(3 or 4 minutes)

A tourist agency is planning an advertising campaign to encourage people to visit Britain. You have been asked for your views about the attractions which should be featured in the campaign. Talk about the six attractions shown on page 142 and decide which **three** should be included. Consider not only the ones which appeal to you and your partner but also those which might appeal to tourist of different ages and from different countries. Try to suggest **one** or **two** more attractions – perhaps ones which are less obvious.

Phase D

(3 or 4 minutes)

In this phase the examiner would ask you to report your decisions and ideas and then ask a few questions to continue the discussion about travel and tourism.

Summarise and explain to your 'examiner' the conclusions you reached. If you want to practise your reporting skills further, work with another pair and take it in turns to report your conclusions.

PRACTICE TEST

5

Answer **all** questions

First text/questions 1–24

Answer questions *1–24* by referring to the information leaflet about fire extinguishers on page *117*.

For questions *1–6* answer by choosing from the possible types of fires in the list *A–D*.

Note: Class A fires = Solids: wood, cloth, paper, plastics ,etc.
   Class B fires = Liquids: paint, petrol, etc.

Which types of fire are the following extinguishers suitable for?

Water	**1**	**A**	Only Class A fires
Multi-purpose dry powder	**2**	**B**	Only Class B fires
Halon	**3**	**C**	Class B and some Class A fires
Foam	**4**	**D**	Both Class A and Class B fires
Carbon dioxide	**5**		
Fire blanket	**6**		

For questions 7–14, answer by choosing from the list of fire extinguishers A–F below.
Note: When more than one answer is required, you may give the answers in any order.

Which fire extinguishers put out the fire by the following methods?	**A** Water
	B Multi-purpose dry powder
Cooling **7** **8**	**C** Halon
Knocking down the flame **9** **10**	**D** Foam
Smothering the fire **11** **12**	**E** Carbon Dioxide
13 .... **14**	**F** Fire Blanket

For questions 15–24 answer by choosing from the types of fire extinguishers A–F listed below.

Which fire extinguishers emit dangerous fumes? **15** **16**	**A** Water
Which extinguisher is suitable for chip pan fires? **17**	**B** Multi-purpose dry powder
Which extinguishers are safe to use on electrical fires? **18** .... **19** **20**	**C** Halon
	D Foam
The fire may start again after using certain extinguishers. Which ones? **21** .... **22** **23**	**E** Carbon dioxide
	F Fire Blanket
Which extinguisher is not suitable for using at home? **24**	

117

Type	Colour code*	How it puts out fires	Best for	How to Use
Water	Red	Mainly by cooling burning material.	Class A fires involving solids. **Danger:** Do not use on live electrical appliances or on burning fat or oil such as chip pan fires.	Point the jet at the base of the flames and keep it moving across the fire. Seek out any hot spots after the main fire is out.
Multi-purpose dry powder	Blue	Knocks down flames and, on burning solids, melts to form a skin smothering the fire. Some cooling effect.	Class A fires involving solids and Class B fires involving liquids. Safe on live electrical equipment although does not penetrate the spaces in equipment easily and the fire may flare up again. Do **not** use on chip pan fires.	Point the jet or discharge horn at the base of the flames and, with a rapid sweeping motion, drive the fire towards the far edge until all the flames are out. If the extinguisher has a shut-off control wait until the air clears and, if you can still see the flame, attack the fire again. **Warning:** Smouldering material in deep-seated fires such as upholstery or bedding can cause the fire to start up again.
Halon 1211 (BCF)	Green	Vaporising liquified gas giving rapid flame knockdown by chemically inhibiting combustion.	Class B fires involving liquids. Clean and light, can also be used on small surface-burning Class A fires involving solids. Effective and safe on live electrical equipment. Ideal for use in cars. Do **not** use on chip pan fires.	**Warning:** This type of extinguisher does not cool the fire very well and you need to watch out that the fire does not start up again. **Danger:** Fumes from Halon 1211 (BCF) extinguishers can be harmful to the user in confined spaces or if used on hot metal: ventilate the area as soon as the fire has been controlled.
Foam	Cream	Forms a blanket of foam over the surface of a burning liquid and smothers the fire. **But:** it is difficult to apply a blanket of foam safely with ordinary foam extinguishers and these are **not** generally recommended for home use.	Class B fires involving liquids. **Warning: Not** suitable for all liquids – check the instructions. Do **not** use on chip pan fires.	Do not aim the jet straight into the liquid. Where the liquid on fire is in a container, point the jet at the inside edge of the container or on a nearby surface above the burining liquid. Allow the foam to build up and flow across the liquid.
Carbon Dioxide CO_2	Black	Vaporising liquified gas which smothers flames by displacing oxygen in the air.	Class B fires involving liquids. Do **not** use on chip pan fires. Clean, effective and safe on live electrical equipment.	**Warning:** This type of extinguisher does not cool the fire very well and you need to watch out the fire does not start up again. **Danger:** Fumes from CO_2 extinguishers can be harmful to user in confined spaces: ventilate the area as soon as the fire has been controlled.
Fire Blanket		Smothering.	Class A fires involving solids and Class B fires involving liquids. Good for small fires in clothing and chip pans provided the blanket completely covers the fire.	Place carefully over fire. Keep your hands shielded from the fire. Do not waft the fire towards you.

Second text/questions 25–33

Read the following newspaper article and then answer the questions on page **120**.

NO DRIVING instructor would tell a learner: jump in, drive away and I'll tell you later how you've done. No coach would promise a new tennis player stroke practice once a match was over. Yet every year trainee teachers are propelled into class-rooms with only the promise of an assessment *after* the lesson they are giving, rather than guidance before or during it.

Dr Peter Tomlinson, a psychologist in Leeds University's school of education, believes the idea of the post-lesson debriefing is flawed. His new method, which bears a closer resemblance to that of the driving instructor, is radio-controlled teacher training: a system of monitoring using microphones, earpieces and transmitters which he calls RAP – radio-assisted practice.

To RAP, tutor and student each wear an earpiece, a four-inch two-way radio which can be hidden under a jacket, and a tiny micro-phone. The student wears the microphone on his or her clothes, so the tutor can hear what both student and nearby children are saying, The tutor straps his micro-phone on to a finger, so that he can unobtrusively speak into it directions, reminders, hints, criticisms and encouragement – all heard only through the student's earpiece.

It sounds complicated and distracting, Dr Tomlinson agrees, and most tutors who have tried it find they have to think harder about what they should be advising students to do, because they must be concise and clear. All but a handful of students quickly adjust to the tutor's interventions, on average every two to four minutes.

Sue Brown (not her real name) is in her second teaching practice of a Postgraduate Certificate of Education. She explained Dr Tomlinson's presence and wiring to her class of inner-city 10-year-olds by saying he was studying how teachers teach. It was her sixth day

High-tech practice as the tutor preaches

Novice teachers can now get on-the-job coaching via an invisible earpiece. Karen Gold investigates

in school: long enough for her to discover that her charges were accustomed to control by criticism and shouting. Her aim for herself as a teacher was to resort to neither.

For art-and-craft she had brought in magazines, food packets and dried pulses for the children to make pictures on the theme of food. Before the lesson, she and Dr Tomlinson discussed how she would introduce the activity and agreed on their focus for RAPping: her positioning in the classroom, vital when children are spread around tables rather than lined behind desk; "scanning", or actively looking everywhere to see what children are doing; keeping the initiative, and not just reacting to attention-seeking or disruption.

At 11 am the children start on their pictures. Within minutes, half a dozen are wandering around. "If you want them at the tables, get them there and reiterate the rules," Dr Tomlinson says. Sue does. They settle. She moves around the class-room, squeezing between tables, stopping frequently. "Positioning," warns her tutor. She shifts to the wall side of the table, so she can see every child.

At 11.25, after a few interruptions, all is reasonably quiet. Even two notorious problem boys are absorbed. "Catch them being good,"

Dr Tomlinson says. Sue moves towards their table to reward their good behaviour with praise.

Before she gets there, a fight breaks out between two girls at another table, Sue defuses it but the calm is broken. Children start wandering around or squabbling. "Get them back on task," Dr Tomlinson says. "Will you all just sit down," Sue shouts, breaking a res-olution. Then she hesitates. "Keep going," the voice urges in her ear-piece, "Next time you won't be able to do this," she threatens. The chil-dren sit down sullenly, "Next time, nip it in the bud a bit earlier and tell them what *to do*, not what *not* to," Dr Tomlinson advises. "You're soldiering on well." Sue grimaces. Two minutes later her tutor is on the earpiece again: "Scan. Scan the middle. There's a lot of kicking going on in the middle."

Sue, who is cutting more paper and trying to interest a boy who has done nothing so far, moves to stop the kicking and misses the dried-pea battle under way nearby. A boy ignores her order to move to another table. "Make sure he does it," Dr Tomlinson says. Sue does. "What should they be doing?" he prompts. Sue, sounding desperate, continues: "Will everybody just listen … Calm down …" Dr Tomlinson addresses her again: "Help them calm down by reminding them what they should be doing,"

The lesson continues chaotically until the end when, at Dr Tom-linson's suggestion, Sue manages to get the children sitting down and dismisses them table by table.

From The Independent on Sunday

25 The new system of radio-assisted practice (RAP) is designed to

- **A** speed up teacher training.
- **B** make teacher training more effective.
- **C** cut the cost of teaching practice.
- **D** make teaching practice less frightening.

26 A problem tutors have found with the system is that they

- **A** aren't used to giving advice briefly.
- **B** have to speak quite loudly.
- **C** can't hear what the children are saying.
- **D** find it hard to think of any advice to give.

27 Most students have found the system

- **A** rather distracting.
- **B** very helpful.
- **C** a bit annoying.
- **D** easy to get used to.

28 Sue Brown's aim for the lesson was to

- **A** control the children without raising her voice.
- **B** be concise and clear.
- **C** avoid being criticised by her tutor.
- **D** keep the pupils entertained during the lesson.

29 It was agreed that one focus of the RAP communication was to be

- **A** positioning the pupils round tables.
- **B** dealing with bad behaviour.
- **C** getting the pupils' attention.
- **D** being aware of everyone in the class.

30 Soon after the start of the lesson, Sue's tutor reminds her

- **A** to move the tables.
- **B** to stand where she can see everyone.
- **C** to go and answer pupils' questions.
- **D** to keep moving round the classroom

31 When the class is quiet, Sue's tutor suggests she goes to two problem boys to

- **A** check that they are really working.
- **B** give them prizes for behaving well.
- **C** tell them how good they are.
- **D** move them to different tables.

32 Later, Sue is too busy to notice

- **A** a pupil who needs help.
- **B** a boy who doesn't obey her.
- **C** children starting to fight.
- **D** children doing nothing

33 At the end of the lesson,

- **A** the children are out of control.
- **B** the children leave in an orderly way.
- **C** Sue talks to the trouble-makers.
- **D** Sue's tutor talks to the class.

Third text/questions 34–39

*For questions **34–39** choose which of the paragraphs **A–G** match the numbered gaps in a newspaper article. There is one extra paragraph, which does not belong in any of the gaps.*

Why Western Australia's Aborigines are speaking Portuguese

From The *Sydney Morning Herald.*

The discovery of Portuguese words in the language of two Aboriginal tribes in Western Australia has raised the possibility that Portuguese sailors came ashore and had contact with Aborigines as long ago as the 1500s.

34

Dr Carl von Brandenstein, a retired West Australian linguist who has spent years researching the theory, claims to have detected almost 50 Portuguese words or derivatives in the vocabularies of the Ngarluma and Karriera tribes, who share a strip of coast between Dampier and Port Hedland.

35

There are also similarities between the Portuguese word for picture, *pintura*, and the Aboriginal word for rock carving, *pintjura*, while hill is *monte* in Portuguese, compared to *marnta*.

36

The Ngarluma and Karriera people use Portuguese words for everday things such as turtles, fire, heart, rib, honey, elbow, spouse and beast. Dr von Brandenstein reasoned that the Aborigines would not have adopted such words unless the Portuguese had been part of the tribe's everyday life. The most likely explanation, he says, is that a Portuguese ship was wrecked on the coast there and that a large number of Portuguese men on board, perhaps 100 or more, survived and were eventually accepted into the local Aboriginal community.

37

The fact that a number of stone balls were known to have been in the possession of local Aborigines for many years seemed to provide another clue. The stones were believed to be granite cannon balls from the Portuguese shipwreck.

38

Last month, the Western Australian Maritime Museum, which has taken an interest in Doctor von Brandenstein's findings, sent an expedition to Depuch Island, west of port Hedland, but it found no trace of a wreck and discovered that one stone ball was dolerite, which is local, and not granite.

39

Dr von Brandenstein conceded yesterday that this was a setback, but he insisted it did not in any way compromise the linguistic evidence he has collected of a Portuguese presence in the north-west of Australia, probably hundreds of years ago.

A He speculated that the Portuguese married Aborigines and that their children grew up with some knowledge of their fathers' language.

B For instance, the Portuguese word for turtle (traditionally, a primary source of food for Aborigines in the area) is *tartaruga*, while the local Aboriginal word for it is pronounced *thatharuga*.

C If they had been found to be cannon balls, they would have dated the wreck to the 16th century.

D The six or so Portuguese words in the language of the Arnhem Land tribe of Aborigines were acquired only indirectly from traders.

E It was concluded that the stones had been shaped into spheres by a purely natural process.

F According to one theory, a Portuguese ship may have been wrecked on the coast and its crewmen, finding themselves marooned, made friends and stayed with the Aborigines.

G Dr von Brandenstein says he has identified other peculiarities in local Aboriginal speech. For instance, most Aboriginal languages have a so-called ergative sentence construction, in which the emphasis is always on the object of the action. The Ngarluma and Karriera languages are unique in Western Australia, he says, in allowing both active and passive constructions similar to European languages.

Fourth text/questions 40–50

Answer questions **40–50** by referring to the newspaper article on page **123**. Choose your answers from cities **A–F**, which are mentioned in the article.

Note: When more than one answer is required, these may be given **in any order.**

A	Birmingham	**D**	Los Angeles
B	Glasgow	**E**	Rome
C	London	**F**	Tokyo

In which city or cities did the researchers receive the best service

in a petrol station? **40** ....

having a telephone installed? **41** ....

having a washing machine delivered? **42** ....

In which city

did a researcher find long queues in a supermarket? **43** ....

did a researcher find a long queue in a bank? **44** ....

was there a problem with a bank's computer? **45** ....

was there a special offer on the price of a washing machine? **46** ....

might a bank pay you? **47** ....

are banking services least efficient? **48** ....

could you wait the longest time for a telephone to be installed? **49** ....

could you spend the longest time waiting for a washing machine to be delivered? **50** ....

• *You want your new washing machine delivered on Monday. Will you get it? We tried in three continents. Here are the results.*

Welcome to Birmingham, the friendliest city in the world.

Fresh flowers are everywhere. The road sweepers carry tourist information so they can tell you what's on at the theatre. The taxi drivers are learning languages. Nightclub bouncers are being taught politeness at the polytechnic. Because one year's visitors are worth a billion pounds, the city wants to offer the finest service in the world.

But we are not visitors.

We are in Currys, the electrical shop, trying to buying a washing machine. The assistant is explaining why it cannot be delivered at a convenient time. His eyes, which look somewhere else, are bored. "The drivers make their own schedules," he says. "We can't tell them what to do. If we said a specific time for you, we'd have to do the same for everyone."

One of the cashiers is talking to her boyfriend. When a customer asks about a television, she rolls her eyes. To whispers and giggles, the customer goes.

Two examples of service, in a city that's trying hard.

So is Britain really bad at service? Last week we carried out an informal survey across the world. There were some examples of obliging, friendly service to our reporters, who posed as customers making slightly awkward demands. Generally, however, standards were lower than in the United States or Japan.

Here are some of the findings from a variety of tasks. They reflect the expectations and temperaments of the countries concerned:

Task: in a typical restaurant, change your entire order after five minutes (even if the food has already arrived).
Tokyo: Waiter grimaced slightly (more in concern than annoyance), excused himself and hurried off. Returned a few minutes later with the amended order.
Los Angeles: Waitress, an actress cracks jokes about pasta being bad for the waistline, and takes fresh order without irritation.
Birmingham: Performed with a smile (at Jeffersons in Hagley Road). When the vegetable dip arrived and our reporter said he wanted a cheese and bacon boat instead, the replacement was served within minutes. "No problem at all," said waitress Sarah Lowe. "And of course you won't have to pay for the dip – our aim is to please."

Buy some shopping in a busy supermarket, Queue. Discover you do not have enough money and ask to put some items back.
Rome: Cashier has no reaction and does not look at customer. Cancels bill and starts again, omitting one item. When customer apologises profusely, replies with neutral voice: "It was no problem."
Tokyo: Cashier polite. No sense of recrimination. In fact, no real reaction at all.
Los Angeles: No problem. Supermarkets are open 24 hours a day, seven days a week. In Von's supermarkets, which have a policy of opening a new till whenever three people queue, the 20,000 staff are trained to listen, nod, and make eye contact, "It also comes in useful in their private lives," the store says.
London: (at Sainsbury's, Nine Elms). Cashier,

SERVICE WITHOUT A SMILE

unfazed, smiles and offers to place shopping in cold store, allowing reporter to return later with cash, or deduct some items if he wishes. But the queues are 10 minutes long and 16 of the 37 tills are unattended.

Ask for another counter to be opened to shorten the lunchtime queue at the bank.
Los Angeles: Wells Fargo promises to credit $5 to your account if there are more than two in the queue, whatever the time of day.
Rome: Three of the six tellers' windows unmanned. One teller on the telephone and when he finishes conversation, hangs a sign: "Window non-operative."

Reporter told he cannot make a deposit because the computer is down, and bank shuts in five minutes (at 1.30pm). User asks if deposit can be done by hand. Teller panics, suspecting reporter to he a lunatic, but eventually agrees.
Tokyo: Even a simple transaction can take half an hour or more, because everything is processed with customer present. People with legitimate inquiries treated poorly by Western standards, because banking in Japan is regarded as above question. Neither friendly nor efficient.
Birmingham: (Barclays, Colmore Row). All tills open except the "quick service" counter. Lengthy queue. Response to reporter's request to open remaining counter: "Sorry, we haven't got any staff available at the moment."

Order a washing machine and ask for delivery between noon and 2pm on Monday.
Tokyo: Shop offers 10% discount and will deliver at any specified time during opening hours (from 9am to 8pm)
Los Angeles: (Sears Roebuck, America's largest department store group): Breathless man, sounding harassed, answers washer department's direct

line and replies: "Don't deliver Sunday 'n' Monday only Tuesday to Saturday 8 to 12, 12 to 5, 6 to 9, I can guarantee delivery within those three times but not outside them."
Birmingham (Currys): Evidently well-rehearsed monologue about how delivery time could not be specified or guaranteed, just morning or afternoon.
Glasgow (Clydesdale, Great Western Road): Could not even say whether morning or afternoon, must stay in all day.

Comet in Dumbarton Road was better: Could not deliver on Monday, only Tuesday – or on Sunday.

How long must you wait to have a telephone installed? Can it be dome between noon and 2pm on Monday?
Tokyo: from four days to one week. No.
Rome: Depends on where you live and who you know. For some (with friends) it's a week; for others (in the central district) a year. This year the telephone company promised that the delay would be brought down to three months, but that claim is unproven. No.
Birmingham: At least eight days "to process the application". (In some parts of London, however, it can take months.) No.
Los Angeles: "Hello, it's Linda, how may I help you?" Reporter asks for telephone between noon and 2pm. "Which Monday? We can connect you as soon as you want, but we only guarantee 8am to noon or noon to 5pm. But if I want it close to 2pm I'm sure the installation department will try."

Drive into a petrol station and ask to have your windscreen cleaned, tyre pressure and oil checked.
Tokyo: It is normal in Japan for petrol station attendants to clean windscreens and empty ashtrays without being asked. Oil and tyres checked efficiently.
Rome: Windscreens are cleaned by hundreds of Polish refugees awaiting immigration papers.
Birmingham: At the Mobil "service" station on Stratford Road, the assistant looks astonished. jokes: "Have you got a disabled sticker then?"

Why does Britain accept standards of service that are lower than they might be? When Tom King was Employment Secretary, he was so concerned at the question that he asked a sociologist, Ray Pahl of Kent university. Pahl thinks it is historical: something to do with class we consider it *servile* to serve.

"Some countries that were rather feudal much later than Britain, like the Mediterranean countries Italy and France, have brilliant service," Pahl says "Often the waiters are better than the customers."

From *The Sunday Times*

Instructions to candidates

*This paper contains one Section A task and four Section B tasks. You must complete the Section A task and **one** task from Section B.*

The two sections carry equal marks.

*Read the task instructions and consider the information **carefully** both for Section A and the task you select for Section B.*

Section A

1   You work for an international hotel which would like to attract more English guests. As an English speaker, you have been asked by the Public Relations Manager to help produce a new publicity leaflet in English.

Read the extract from the Public Relations Manager's memo and the current publicity information and then, **using the information carefully**, write the text for the new leaflet and the memo described in the instructions on page 125.

Where I'd like your help is with the new publicity leaflet. The current information sheet has the basic facts but it's very brief and it's also a bit out of date now – I've made a note of changes which should be incorporated. Could you rewrite it in more detail and in a way that catches people's attention and really *sells* the hotel? One other point – we'll need some better photographs. Could you send a memo to Paul B, the hotel photographer, and ask him to take some new shots (in colour) which will do the hotel more justice? Maybe you could suggest a few suitable locations to him?

The Hotel Continental

* established in 1956 — *recently renovated.*

* waterfront location
    20 mins from airport
* near railway station and university

* 82 bedrooms all pleasantly furnished, *(most)* *all*
    with private bathrooms, radio and telephone
    + colour TVs
* restaurant with good reputation

* conference facilities for 100 people
    Good Eating Guide award last year
* private car park

* large garden

* efficient service
* *Special weekend rates*

Write (a) the text for the new **publicity leaflet** as requested by the Public Relations Manager (approximately 200 words)

(b) a relevant **memo** to Paul B, the hotel photographer, (approximately 50 words)

Section B

Choose **ONE** *of the following writing tasks. Your answer should follow exactly the instructions given. Write approximately 250 words.*

2 An English friend is going to spend a weekend in a town or city which you know well. This is part of a letter which you receive.

As you're a bit of an expert, I'm hoping you can give me lots of advice about where to go and what to see in my short stay (remember I've only got a weekend!) I'd also like to know what not to do and where not to go – the tourist traps to avoid etc. Are there any local specialities I should make a point of trying when I'm eating out? Oh, and by the way, have you any idea of what the weather will be like at this time of year? Let me know if I need to pack sunglasses or an extra sweater!

Write to your friend, giving **practical advice**, referring to the points in the letter.

3 Your school or college has an English Circle which meets once a week but attendance has been poor lately and the meetings may have to end unless new members can be found. Write **an article** for the students' magazine describing the activities of the group and encouraging new members to join.

4 You have just seen the following advertisement.

Do you enjoy travelling?
Do you get on well with children?

Alpha Airlines is looking for responsible young people to act as escorts for children aged between 5 and 12 who are travelling unaccompanied on international flights.
Escorts are needed to supervise children (individually or in groups of up to six) from their departure until they are met at their destination.
   You will need to be level-headed and resourceful, and some experience of looking after children is essential.
   To apply for this well-paid and rewarding work, please write giving details of why you think you would be suitable, with the names of two referees to:

Personnel Officer, Alpha Airlines, Huntley, Berks.

Write your **application** for this position giving relevant information about yourself.

5 You work as an assistant in an office or as an au-pair in an English-speaking family. You have been given permission to have a day off in order to attend an important family occasion but only on condition that you can find someone to replace you for the day. Fortunately a good friend has offered to help out. Write **a set of instructions** for your friend explaining exactly what he/she will have to do during the day.

Answer **all** questions.

Section A

1   *For questions 1–15, read the article below and circle the letter next to the word which best fits each space. The exercise begins with an example (0).*

FLYING PIGEONS FOREVER

Bikes are best – in China they are a way of life, at the hub of a wheel that reaches round the Third World.

Pedal, chain, wheels and frame – the basic (0) .....*design*..... of the bicycle is as near perfect as a machine can be. And bikes are good for you, too. For every person who takes a

(1) .... by bike rather than by car there is less pollution, less fuel used, less

(2) .... taken on the road and one healthier person.

   The world's 800 million bicycles (3) .... cars by two to one and almost half of

them are in China. In the US there are fewer bicycles than cars (4) .... in China there

are 250 times as many! Between them, the 'Flying Pigeon' factory in Tianjin and the 'Forever'

factory in Shanghai (5) .... almost seven million bicycles every year. The parts are

(6) .... in kit form to be (7) .... by hundreds of local distributors. So

employment in the bicycle industry is (8) .... widely across the country. The factory

work, though relatively clean and healthy, is repetitive and unrewarding. (9) ....,

people who work with bicycles seem to share a common sense of endeavour.

   The 'Flying Pigeon' factory exports to 32 countries, particularly to the Third World where

sturdy, durable design and low-cost components are (10) .... China makes all the

bicycles sold in Bangladesh, where they are an important working tool and the basic

(11) .... of transport for millions of people.

   Industrial countries have as many bikes per (12) .... as in Asia, but

(13) .... to use them less. The citizens of Groningen in the Netherlands, however,

make half their daily trips by bike – more even than in Beijing, China. Tianjin, home of the

'Flying Pigeon', (14) .... the world league, with three-quarters of daily trips made by

bike. That may not (15) .... the people of Tianjin the happiest and healthiest in the

world – but it should help.

From The New Internationalist

126

0	**A** shape	**B** plan	**C** pattern	**(D)** design
1	**A** journey	**B** travel	**C** trip	**D** drive
2	**A** area	**B** space	**C** place	**D** distance
3	**A** outnumber	**B** outweigh	**C** overtake	**D** overcome
4	**A** as	**B** while	**C** unlike	**D** compared
5	**A** invent	**B** create	**C** process	**D** produce
6	**A** sent for	**B** sent on	**C** sent out	**D** sent in
7	**A** assembled	**B** connected	**C** joined	**D** combined
8	**A** situated	**B** spread	**C** expanded	**D** set
9	**A** Although	**B** Despite	**C** Nevertheless	**D** Furthermore
10	**A** special	**B** major	**C** key	**D** essential
11	**A** means	**B** medium	**C** way	**D** service
12	**A** man	**B** head	**C** body	**D** hand
13	**A** try	**B** enjoy	**C** require	**D** tend
14	**A** beats	**B** climbs	**C** tops	**D** passes
15	**A** result in	**B** lead to	**C** make	**D** be

2 *For questions **16–30**, complete the following article by writing the missing words in the spaces provided. **Use only one word in each space.** The exercise begins with an example (**0**).*

Skiing at the limits

Screaming, Jonathan Elabor hurls himself (**0**) ....*in*........ a straight line down the side of a mountain. (**16**) .... seconds, he is travelling at 209 kilometres an hour. (**17**) .... he can hear is his heart pounding at 210 beats a minute, and the hiss of the air over his skin-tight Lycra suit. "It's like   jumping from a high board (**18**) .... knowing whether the water's there   at the bottom," he says. Elabor is Britain's number one speed skier - a player in the latest, and some say craziest, addition (**19**) .... the winter sports scene.

The speed skier (**20**) .... plunging down a kilometre or more of a mountainside faster than a free-falling parachutist. He's heading (**21**) .... a 100-metre-long timed stretch. Radar guns (**22**) .... measure his speed as he flashes by in less than a second. The record, (**23**) .... by Monaco's Michael Prufer, is 228 kilometres an hour – which is more than twice as fast as the legal speed limit (**24**) .... travelling inside the protective steel cage of a car in the UK.

Speed skiing, (**25**) .... motor racing, is a sport driven by technology. In fact, the technology is similar - (**26**) .... use advanced materials developed for the aerospace business, and aerodynamics carefully researched in wind tunnels. (**27**) .... speed skiers are not surrounded by a million-pound car and a huge team of engineers. They're (**28**) .... their own.

Travelling twice as fast as the more familiar downhill ski racers, speed skiers have to resort to the ultimate in aerodynamics. Reducing their air resistance (**29**) .... only 10 per cent as they swoop down the mountain (**30**) .... add 16 km/hour to the top speed – often the difference between first place and fourth.

From *Focus* magazine

3 In the following text (Questions *31–46*) some lines have one word **omitted.** Write the missing word in the space provided. In some lines there is an **unnecessary** word. Cross out the unnecessary word and write it in the space provided. Some lines are correct. Indicate each of these lines with a tick (√). The first **three** lines have been done as examples.

HOW TO HAVE A BABY AND SAVE YOUR CAREER

0	...to...	Britain's businesswomen have been told they must t̸o̸ nurse
0	...with...	their careers along their babies if they want to get to the top.
0	...√...	The advice came from a panel of seven top women executives
31	....	at a London seminar on the women at work. Businesswomen
32	....	were advised keep a high profile while on maternity leave if
33	....	they wanted to hold on to their jobs. They should keep in
34	....	regular touch with their bosses looking after their babies. Eve
35	....	Newbold, one of the speakers, said: "I've got one woman on
36	....	maternity leave at the moment phones me up every week and
37	....	tells me if she wants her job back. That makes it much harder
38	....	for anyone not to forget her."
39	....	The seminar, entitled "Danger! Women at Work" and attended
40	....	by more 300 businesswomen, was told that women must have
41	....	a major change in attitude if they were stand a chance of
42	....	winning the battle of the sexes at work. The panel called for
43	....	more child care of facilities and for the responsibility of raising
44	....	children to shared more equally between the sexes. Catherine
45	....	James, strategy and planning director at Grand Metropolitan,
46	....	said: "Why is child care such a female issue? We not solve the
		problem until men start to ask the same questions as we do."

4 For questions *47–61*, read the following informal note and use the information in it to complete the numbered gaps in the letter to your landlord. **Use no more than two words for each gap.** The exercise begins with an example (**0**). The words which you need **do not** occur in the informal note.

Dear Sarah,

Just a note to let you know my new address, though I'm afraid it may be a temporary one! My brother fixed up this accommodation for me while I was away, as you know, but I don't suppose he had time to look the place over very thoroughly and of course the landlord didn't mention any problems! Anyway, it was quite a shock when I arrived – the carpets in the living room are dirty and stained, one of the kitchen tap drips all the time, a window pane is broken and, worst of all, there's a smell of gas from the cooker, which could be really dangerous. I'm writing to the landlord to ask him to sort things out as soon as possible. If he won't agree, the only thing I can do is contact the local council. Wish me luck!

Love H.

Dear Mr Stubbs,

<u>Top Floor Flat, 25 St Helen's Road</u>

I have recently (0) .....<u>moved into</u>..... the above property and I'm writing to (47) ....
of a number of problems which require urgent (48) .... Although my brother
(49) .... the flat on my (50) .... , he obviously wasn't (51) ....
of these problems and, if they had been (52) .... out to him, he certainly would not
have signed the rental agreement.
The two most (53) .... problems are the gas cooker which appears to have a gas
(54) .... and therefore represents a potentially serious (55) .... hazard,
and a broken window pane which needs (56) .... for reasons of security. In addition,
the carpet in the living room needs (57) .... , and there's also a tap in the kitchen
which drips (58) ....
I trust you will (59) .... the necessary repairs without (60) .... If not,
I will have no (61) .... but to contact the local council.

        Yours sincerely,

5   For questions **62–66**, read through the following text and then choose from the list **A–I** the best
     phrase or sentence given below to fill each of the blanks. Write one letter (**A–I**) in each space.
     Some of the suggested answers do not fit at all. One answer has been given as an example (**0**),

Adapting to the climate – cold comforts and hot sweats

From the poles to the tropics, weather determines the way we live. Most cultures have developed
technology to conquer the elements – (**0**) ..<u>G</u>. . Eskimos have learned to cope with temperatures
that drop to –50°C. They pile on layers of clothes and retreat to the insulation of their igloos
(**62**) ....

The average Eskimo has a metabolic rate 30 per cent higher than the average European. But
this is the result of a diet low in carbohydrates and high in protein and fat – (**63**) ..... . It is
quickly lost if the diet is changed. Eskimos have also evolved short arms and legs so they have
less surface area to radiate heat. People living in the tropics who are acclimatised to heat have a
larger blood volume, enabling them to radiate heat more effectively. In a hot dry climate sweating is the best way for the body (64) ..... . But in the tropics, where there is high humidity,
increasing sweat production may offer no advantage (**65**) ..... . Acclimatisation to heat encour-
ages a tendency for salt concentrations in sweat to decrease. Nigerians, for example, lose signifi-
cantly less salt (**66**) ..... than British men. This specific adaptation to the climate is due to
increases in the concentration of a hormone called aldosterone in the blood, which acts on the
sweat glands and the kidneys to aid conservation of salt.

                                                        From *Focus* magazine

A   through sweating
B   helping them to work more efficiently
C   not because they were born with this advantage
D   because sweat does not evaporate
E   to reduce their body temperature
F   for warmth
G   using clothing, housing and food to adapt to extremes of climate
H   by dressing up warmly
I   to lose excess heat

6 *You have been asked to prepare an information sheet about a holiday. Read the notes below and use the notes to prepare the information sheet. Write **no more than one sentence** for each numbered set of notes, using connecting words and phrases as appropriate. You may add words and change the form of words given in the notes but do not add any extra information. The first point has been expanded for you as an example (**0**).*

TOUR TS 1215

0 **CHECK-IN** Report Skyways check-in desk (Terminal 3) – 2hrs before dep. time (min.).

67 **LUGGAGE** Ensure each piece carries Skyways label – clearly marked name, address (BLOCK CAPITALS).

68 **FLIGHT** Skyways Airbus departs 10.25 am – light lunch served during flight (2hr 10 min).

69 **TRANSFER** Welcome reception at airport before – coaches depart short drive to Concorde Hotel – 7 days' accommodation booked.

70 **PHOTOGRAPHY** Films available hotel – choice very limited – suggest purchase films before travel (same applies if camera needs batteries).

71 **WHAT TO WEAR** Daytime: light clothing (natural fibres) recommended
Evening: smart casual clothing (no shorts or swimwear).

72 **SHOPPING** Free time for shopping in town Thursday & Saturday – travel reps will advise best places and bargains.

73 **TIPPING** Included for all meals in tour – not guides or bus drivers – suggest max. 12 dollars each (end of tour).

The Directors and Staff of Skyways Holidays
would like to wish you a most enjoyable holiday

TOUR TS 1215

0 Please report to the Skyways check-in desk in Terminal 3 approximately 2 hours before departure time and present your ticket to the airline staff.

67

68

69

70

71

72

72

73

Section A

You will hear an advertisement which mentions special savings on several items of household equipment. For questions 1–12, complete the table by filling in the missing information.

You will hear the recording twice.

GREAT SAVINGS

Product	Features	Sale Price	Saving	Special Offer
Colour TV	21 cm **1** [ ] + remote control	£499	£50	Free **2** [ ]
Video Recorder	remote control + **3** [ ]	**4** [ ]	£40	10 free video cassettes
5 [ ]	12 place settings	£369	£10	**6** [ ] – ask for details
Cooker	**7** [ ] + ceramic hob	£649	£150	Chance of a **8** [ ] – ask for details
Chest Freezer	**9** [ ] model	£369	**10** [ ]	Free watch
11 [ ]	Built-in tools	£99	£15	Free **12** [ ]

131

You will hear the some advice on complaining about a holiday. As you listen, you must fill in the information for questions 13–19.

Listen very carefully as you will hear this piece only ONCE.

HOLIDAY COMPLAINTS

While you're away ....

- Try and sort out the problem at the resort. Complain to the company

  13 [_____]

- Take the brochure and a copy of the **14** [_____]

  as evidence of what you've been promised.

  15 [_____] of what you're complaining about.

- Keep all **16** [_____] and take down the names and

  addresses of other dissatisfied holidaymakers.

- Fill in the tour operator's **17** [_____] .

When you return ....

- Write to the company quickly, saying how much **18** [_____]

  you require.

- If you still get nowhere, contact ABTA which offers an independent

  arbitration scheme for a **19** [_____] of about £30.

Section C

You will hear an interview with Mary Dallas, an archaeologist, whose work involves studying aboriginal sites in Australia. For questions 20–29 complete the sentences with an appropriate word or short phrase.
You will hear the piece twice.

Mary enjoys her job because it offers a combination of working outside and

sitting **20** _____ , using her brain.

She spends about **21** _____ of her time away from her

office, working in the field.

She looks for aboriginal sites in places that haven't been disturbed by

22 _____ or suburbs or industry.

Whether she goes out alone or not depends on how rough it's going to be and

whether it might also be **23** _____ .

In rough country, there's a risk of **24** _____ or falling

down a cliff.

Among the animals she might see are different types of **25** _____

She first wanted to be an archaeologist when she was **26** _____ .

She became interested in aboriginal culture while she was

27 _____

Mary would like to have studied more **28** _____ subjects

as part of her degree.

Compared with the past, there are now more **29** _____

studying to be archeologists.

Section D

You will hear five callers on a radio phone-in programme talking about speeches they have heard. You will hear the recording twice.

Task One

*The callers heard the speeches on different occasions. Look at occasions listed **A–H** and put them in the order in which you hear about them by filling in the boxes numbered **30–34**.*

What was the occasion for each speech?

A   a meeting for women

B   a birthday party

C   a debate

D   a wedding

E   a competition

F   a party for someone who was leaving

G   a prize-giving ceremony

H   a school meeting

30	
31	
32	
33	
34	

Task Two

*The callers were impressed by the speeches for different reasons. Look at the list of reasons **A–H** and put them in order by filling in the boxes numbered **35–39**.*

What impressed the caller about the speech?

A   It was amusing.

B   It was strongly felt.

C   It contained a lot of useful facts.

D   It was a good story.

E   It touched the emotions.

F   It was delivered without notes.

G   It led to a lot of questions.

H   It included practical demonstrations.

35	
36	
37	
38	
39	

Work in groups of three. One student should play the role of the examiner, giving instructions, asking further questions and making sure both candidates play an equal part in the conversation.

Phase A

(about 3 minutes)

- Greet the examiner and introduce your partner to them.
- Find out whether your partner enjoys cooking and what their particular likes and dislikes in food are. Tell the others about your tastes in food.
- Tell the others what kind of music you like and whether you play any kind of musical instrument. Find out about your partner's musical tastes.
- Ask your partner about their future plans and ambitions. Explain what yours are.

Phase B

(about 3 or 4 minutes)

Task 1 (Compare and contrast)

In this part of the test you will each have a picture to look at. The pictures are similar but not the same. Don't look at each other's pictures.

Candidate A: Turn to the picture on page 143 and describe what you can see. You have about a minute.

Candidate B: Turn to the picture on page 147 and listen to your partner's description. You can make notes on a piece of paper if you wish. When A has finished, mention **two** things which are the same as, and **two** things which are different from A's picture.

Now compare the two pictures.

Task 2 (Describe and relate)

Candidate B has six pictures. Candidate A has the same pictures but in a different order and also an extra one. Don't look at each other's pictures.

Candidate B: Turn to the set of pictures on page 140. Listen to your partner's description and decide which picture is not described. You may make notes if you wish. When B has finished, describe the remaining picture.

Candidate A: Turn to the set of pictures on page 139. Listen to your partner's description and decide which picture is not described. You may make notes if you wish. When B has finished, describe the remaining picture.

Phase C

(3 or 4 minutes)

Look at the cartoon below and decide what point the cartoonist is making. Discuss what solution there could be to the problem and talk about other sources of noise in modern life which cause problems. Find out what kind of noise your partner dislikes and why.

Phase D

(3 or 4 minutes)

In this phase the examiner would ask you to report the main points from your discussion and also ask a few questions to continue the discussion about noise and noise pollution.

Summarise and explain to your 'examiner' the conclusions you reached. If you want to practise your reporting skills further, work with another pair and take it in turns to report your conclusions.

Test 1 Phase B Task 2 **A**

Test 3 Phase C

Test 3 Phase B Task 1 **B**

Test 4 Phase C

Theatre

Museums/Galleries

Castles and historic houses

Restaurants

Parks and gardens

London sights

Test 3 Phase B Task 2 A

Test 5 Phase B Task 1 A

Any pen can write. This one talks, too ...

The Pencorder is the world's first writing instrument with a built-in digital recorder. Using advanced customised semi-conductor chips, it holds up to 40 seconds of speech - and plays it back with telephone clarity via a miniature loudspeaker that produces very high quality sound.

"Quick, before I forget ... it's E = MC2!"

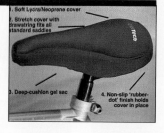

Catch spiders the easy way

This brilliant Spider Catcher lets you scoop up spiders and other unwanted insects and deposit them safely back outside without any harm to the insect, you or your nerves!

Geltech Saddle Cover just £9.95

Here's the instant way to make cycling more comfortable - simply fit the new Geltech Cover on top of your existing saddle. Beneath the neoprene/lycra covering there's a contoured gel sac, approx 1cm thick. Warm in winter and cool in summer,

1. Soft Lycra/Neoprene cover
2. Stretch cover with drawstring fits all standard saddles
3. Deep-cushion gel sac
4. Non-slip 'rubber-dot' finish holds cover in place

Cut down on smoking

Smoke and Stop is a unique electronic locking cigarette box that helps to progressively lengthen the time between cigarettes, so it's easier to gradually cut down. Programme in your chosen time interval (from 15 minutes) and at the end of that time, the box is unlocked automatically.

Ice-Pack Pillow

When you've got a thumping headache, the idea of a soothing cold compress applied to the back of your neck can seem very welcome - and that's just what the British-made Ice-Pack Pillow provides.

Pet Vac — electronic pet grooming

Pet Vac is the new, more effective way to groom cats and dogs. Battery-operated, it incorporates a powerful mini fan to vacuum up hair and loose dirt as you brush, helping to keep your pet's coat clean

Test 3 Phase B Task 2 **B**

Test 4 Phase B Task 1 **B**

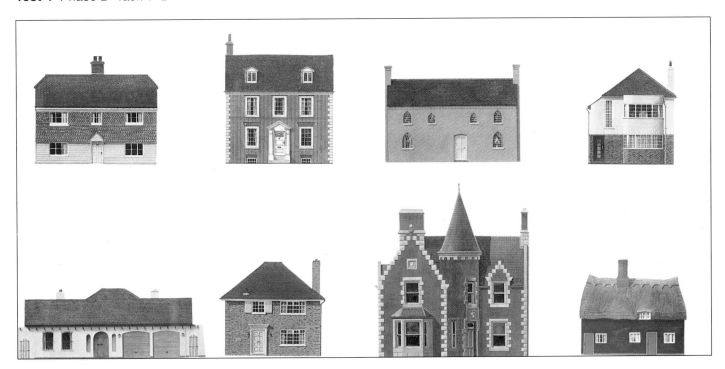

Test 4 Phase B Task 2 **B**

Test 5 Phase B Task 1 **B**

Test 2 Phase B Task 1 **A**

TAPESCRIPTS

Test 1

There are four sections A, B, C and D. You will hear Section B once only. All the other parts of the test will be heard twice. There will be a pause before each part to allow you to look through the questions and other pauses to let you think about your answers.

You should write your answers on the question paper. In the exam you will have ten minutes at the end to transfer your answers to the separate answer sheet.

Section A

You will hear some information about home security. For questions 1–11 complete the table by filling in the missing information. You will hear the recording twice.

Thank you for calling the Goldmark Insurance telephone advice line on home security. I'm Jeremy Kent, customer services manager at Goldmark Insurance, and I'm here with some tips to help you guard against intruders.

Unfortunately, we often make life all too easy for the burglar – a few seconds is all it takes for him to gain entry to a house before making off with a few of the owner's precious possessions. Don't join the crime statistics – check your home security now.

The first line of defence is obviously the doors, all the doors, not just the front door. Most houses have inadequate locks and inadequate locks can be easily opened, so make sure you fit strong, good quality locks to all your outside doors.

Next the windows. Downstairs windows are one of the burglar's favourite methods of entry because they often provide easy access. Again, the solution is to fit strong window locks and there are many different types on the market. This way, even if the burglar breaks a pane of glass, he won't be able to reach in and open the window from the inside.

Upstairs windows may seem less accessible but not so in the case of the determined burglar because they can be reached from the roof or with a ladder. Once again, secure all upstairs windows with strong locks.

There is a type of window which is the burglar's particular favourite and that's the louvre window. These are most often found in bathrooms and kitchens and they have panels of glass which can be raised or lowered from inside. The problem is that the glass panels slide out. So they're an invitation to a burglar, and if you have any windows of that type, the best advice is to fit a lock or, better still, replace with ordinary windows.

The next area to consider is the garage or the garden shed. They're both handy places to keep tools in and that means they can provide useful burglary tools too. There's many a burglar who has been grateful to the householder for this assistance. Use a good padlock on the door or remove tools.

Now the porch. If this is unlit, as is often the case, it means that callers cannot be identified. You have to open the door before you know who it is that's calling, and then it may be too late. You should fit a security light. This is designed to switch on as soon as anyone approaches your front door, even before they ring the doorbell. It's often enough to scare away a potential thief.

Finally, the drain pipe. This provides a means of reaching the upstairs windows. And though it might not look the easiest thing to shin up, there are certainly burglars who would find it very helpful. You can't remove the pipe itself, of course, but the answer here is to secure windows close to the drain pipe.

Thank you for calling the Goldmark Insurance Advice Line on home security.

Now you will hear the piece again.
That is the end of Section A.

Section B

You will hear about a competition for young writers. As you listen, you must fill in the information for questions 12–19. Listen very carefully as you will hear the recording only once.

Now to that competition I mentioned at the beginning of the programme. I'll be giving you details about how to enter in a minute, so have a pencil and piece of paper ready. The Bookworm Young Writer's Competition is open to anyone aged 16 or under on the closing date – I'll tell you when that is later. So if you're in that age group, and you're imaginative and like writing, why not have a go? There are more than fifty prizes and the winning entries will have their work published in a paperback book next year.

So how do you enter? Well, you can submit any original piece of writing whether it's poetry, prose, or even drama. But it must be original. Anything which is a copy or a near copy of something you've read elsewhere will be automatically disqualified. The maximum length for each entry is 3,500 words but, of course, you don't have to write that much or anything like it.

Now, this part is important. Your entry must be accompanied by a signed statement from one of your parents or from your teacher saying that your entry is all your own work and that it was written unaided, that is without any help from anyone. Don't forget to get that statement and make sure it's signed.

If you need to use more than one sheet of paper, make sure the sheets are all clearly numbered and also pinned together. You don't want your brilliant entry coming adrift! When you've got your entry ready, you'll need to send it to: Young Writers' Competition, P.O. Box 2,000, Taunton, Somerset, TA1 5QT. Got that? Young Writers' Competition, P.O. Box 2,000, Taunton, Somerset, TA1 5QT. Oh, and remember to keep a copy of your work because none of the entries will be returned.

Now that all-important closing date. All entries must be received by September 12th. So you've got a whole month to work on your entry. Get writing, and good luck!

That is the end of Section B.

Section B

You will hear an interview with Robert Miles who works as a Flight Service Director for an airline. For questions 20–31 complete the sentences with an appropriate word or short phrase. You will hear the piece twice.

Interviewer: Can I ask you what the good parts of the job are?

Robert Miles: The good parts are the travelling to different areas of the world and looking after different people on board the aircraft.

Interviewer: And what about the bad parts? Are they looking after not so nice people?

Robert Miles: No, that's part and parcel of the job. You've got to adapt to looking after good people as well as bad people. I guess the bad part would be the long hours that are involved. We do up to sixteen, seventeen hours at a time, and that's probably the hardest part.

Interviewer: And how long have you been doing this job?

Robert Miles: I've been with the company for twenty six years.

Interviewer: Goodness! And how did you come to actually start your career?

Robert Miles: I used to work in the public service. And at that time, the recruitment of flight attendants was very much word of mouth, and one of the guys in the office applied for the job and didn't get it. And he sort of said to me that they were looking for, for people of lesser intelligence so I applied for the job! I managed to get it and I've, it's been great. I've never looked back.

Interviewer: You've never been tempted to leave or do something else?

Robert Miles: Like everybody else, I decided that I'd do it for two years initially, to see the world. But once you get bitten by the bug, that's it and you never seem to get rid of it. And I've never wanted to leave.

Interviewer: How much time do you spend now, say, in a month actually flying?

Robert Miles: What we have is a bid period – that's a working period of fifty six days and you must have a minimum of eighteen days off in fifty six. But the system is pretty complicated and works out on hours, and you can have up to twenty eight days off in a working period if things work out right.

Interviewer: And you spend some time behind a desk as well?

Robert Miles: Yes, I'm attached to Cabin Crew Management and have been for the last three years. It's good because it gives you a chance to see what goes on behind the scenes, particularly with the Customer Relations Department but other departments as well. Whereas the normal crew that fly, continually fly, they never get a chance to see what goes on behind the scenes.

Interviewer: Have you ever had as a passenger anyone particularly famous?

Robert Miles: Yes, I've been lucky enough to be a crew member on two royal flights. I think it was about '73, I managed to do two sectors with the Queen. We brought her out of Vancouver to Honolulu and then from Singapore to Teheran. That was sensational.

Interviewer: And what do you do when you get somebody who's really frightened of flying?

Robert Miles: I think the easiest thing is to reassure them that air travel is probably the safest way to go. I guess you've got more chance of having an accident if you walk across the road. If you can reassure the passenger and stay with them as much as you can, show them how the aircraft works, take them on to the flight deck, let them see what the captain does and what the flight deck crew do. And then explain that the cabin crew are fully trained in safety procedures on board the aircraft, and if anything is going to happen, they're in safe hands.

Interviewer: You've said that it's your job to look after all kinds of passengers, the agreeable ones and the disagreeable ones, but what would you say is the most annoying thing from your point of view in a passenger?

Robert Miles: I guess a passenger who makes completely unreasonable demands, things that just cannot be done on board the aircraft. We always try to help passengers in any way. But there are some passengers who want the impossible. I mean, if we could give them the aircraft they'd probably take it!

Interviewer: You've been doing this job for a long time. What have been the biggest changes in that time in the nature of the work?

Robert Miles: Well I started off on 707 aircraft. Now we're up to the big 747 400 series which carry over 400 people. In the early days the maximum that we carried was 140 and we could give a more personalised service to the passengers. We had a lot more time to talk to people individually. Now it's more of a group discussion where you talk to six or seven people in a row at one time. That's probably the biggest change. Another is flying longer sectors. You know, we now operate from Bangkok straight through to London; we operate Sydney – Los Angeles direct. They're the big changes.

Interviewer: Thanks very much.

Robert Miles: Great.

Now you will hear the piece again.
That is the end of Section C.

Section D

Now look at Section D for the fourth and last part of the test. You will hear five people talking about bargains they have bought. Task one. For questions 32–36 look at the eight pictures labelled A–H. As you listen, put the pictures in order by completing the boxes 32–36 with the appropriate letter. Task two. Letters A–H list possible reasons for people selling things cheaply to the different speakers. Decide which one on the list fits the situation in each case. For questions 37–41 put the letter of the description against the appropriate speaker. You will hear the recording twice.

Yes, it's lovely isn't it? A typical oriental design and I love the colour. I think it's hand-made, actually, but I don't suppose it's valuable or anything. I got it from an aunt of mine. It was on the floor in her hallway, and I said how much I liked it. She looked at me as if I was mad and said, "That old thing? You can have it if you want." She said she'd much rather have a nice modern one to go with the wallpaper. So I bought her a new one quite cheaply and kept this, and we're both happy.

It belonged to somebody I knew at work. He'd ordered it from a catalogue thinking it would be an easy way to lose weight. But it came in kit form and by the time he got it assembled, he'd sort of gone off the whole idea – he said he'd feel stupid sitting pedalling away at it in front of the television – so he never got round to trying it at all. He let me have it quite reasonably. I think it's great!

A friend of mine was going to live abroad and he sold it to me for £50 – he said he didn't have time to put an advert in the paper and all that. I reckon I got a real bargain. That was 3 years ago and it's been going strong ever since. Not a spot of rust anywhere on the bodywork and the interior is immaculate. The only thing I've had to buy is two new tyres.

I was at a jumble sale, wandering around and it caught my eye. I'd been looking for something to put my computer on and it seemed about the right size. It was quite badly scratched but I could see it was beautifully made. If you pull out that drawer in the front, you'll see what I mean. It only cost £10, if I remember rightly. Since then, I've been told it's antique and worth quite a lot more than £10!

My brother was having a clear-out and he offered it to me for a fiver. He didn't use it any more – he's got a word processor now – so it was just taking up valuable space. It's not electric or electronic or anything, just a good old-fashioned manual one – but it works really well. My tutor at college is delighted – he says it takes him half the time to read through one of my essays now.

Now you will hear the piece again.
That is the end the test.

Test 2

Section A

You will hear some information about three different answering machines. For questions 1–23 complete the table by filling in the missing information or by ticking the boxes to indicate what features each machine has. If a machine does not have a particular feature put a cross. Four answers have been given as examples. You will hear the recording twice.

Presenter: Next up in the programme is our consumer slot and today we take a look at three new answering machines and ask what points you should consider when you're choosing a machine. Here's Patricia Kennedy with her report.

Patricia Kennedy: Having an answering machine means that people can get in touch with you even when you're out and they're also a handy way of avoiding calls at times when you're busy or watching your favourite TV programme! Prices vary enormously as do the features which are included, so it's worth comparing models carefully. For example, many machines limit the length of the announcement you make, giving your name, telephone number and so on. Of the three models we tested, the **Cuckoo** is the meanest, with only 15 seconds available for the announcement, the **Budgie** comes next with 30, while the **Vulture** offers a full 120 seconds.

Most machines also give the caller a maximum time to leave their message in. This is the case with the **Budgie**, where it's 60 seconds, and the **Cuckoo** which is a bit more generous with 150 seconds. The **Vulture**, however, gives the caller unlimited time.

After these basics, there are a number of special features which may or not be useful to you. The more expensive models have a system for logging the time and date of each message using a synthesized voice after each recording. Both the **Cuckoo** and the **Vulture** have this feature. Two-way recording of conversations may be useful if you use your phone for business. This is only available on the **Vulture**.

What else? Yes, most answering machines these days allow you to listen to your messages from another telephone by remote control and all three of our test models have this feature.

So, our verdict on the three answering machines we tested? First, the **Budgie** which, appropriately enough, is a budget model. This was easy to use and performed well in most respects except that the recorded announcement was a bit muffled. Good value if you don't need too many features. Next the **Cuckoo** which is quite a bit more expensive but it's worth paying the extra for longer messages and to record time and date. It's also the only model which can be wall-mounted – a useful way of saving space. The **Cuckoo** made very clear recordings but we found the procedure for listening to and saving messages a bit complicated. Finally the **Vulture**: this was child's play to use and the recorded messages were crystal-clear. It has most of the features you'd ever want and does just about everything except make the tea! Even so, we thought it was a bit over-priced.

Presenter: Thank you, Patricia for that report. I've no doubt there will be a model which makes the tea before long ...

Now you will hear the piece again.
That is the end of Section A.

Section B

You will hear a tour guide giving a group of tourists some extra details about their programme. As you listen you must fill in the information for questions 24–31. Listen very carefully as you will hear the recording only once.

Hello everybody. My name is Sally Taylor and on behalf of Goodwill Tours, I'd like to welcome you all to Jordan for your Magic of Petra holiday break. I hope you've had a good journey and you're not feeling too exhausted despite the fact that your flight was delayed. Anyway, as your tour guide it's my job to make sure you have a really wonderful time while you're in Jordan – so if you have any questions or problems, don't hesitate to come and see me. Don't forget, my name is Sally Taylor.

Well, we'll be setting off shortly for our drive to the hotel and in the meantime I'd like to give you some information about the programme. First of all, the bad news! Because of your late arrival this evening, the welcome dinner which is mentioned on your programme has been cancelled. Now, the hotel will be providing sandwiches and fruit, though, so if you're feeling peckish, don't worry!

Tomorrow morning breakfast will be served by the swimming pool. After that there's a coach tour of the city, and coaches will leave the hotel at 9.30. The afternoon is free for relaxing or shopping, but for the energetic ones amongst you, we've organised an optional visit to the gold market. It's one of the most interesting gold markets in the Middle East, in fact, and well worth seeing. In the evening, although it's not mentioned on your programme, we'll be having a buffet dinner and this will be accompanied by musical entertainment. We hope this will make up for the welcome dinner you're missing tonight.

On Tuesday, you'll need to have an early breakfast because this is the big day and our journey to Petra begins at 8.30. Now it's important to choose comfortable clothing to wear because you'll be spending quite a few hours on the coach and the day also includes some horse-riding, of course! The journey takes about three hours and, after your tour of the city, you'll be lunching at the Petra Vista Hotel. We leave Petra at about 4 o'clock and, on the way back, there's another event that's not on your programme. We'll be making a stop for afternoon tea at a Turkish fort.

This is one of several historical Turkish forts in Jordan and it makes a splendid setting for our refreshment stop. In the evening, back at the hotel there's the very special 1001 Arabian Nights dinner.

Finally, as regards your return journey on Wednesday. Coaches will leave for the airport at 10.30 promptly, so could you gather in the hotel lobby please? Your luggage will also be collected from you there. The flight will depart at 12 o'clock noon, all being well. Now, are there any questions?

That is the end of Section B.

Section C

You will hear part of an interview with a sub-editor on a newspaper. For questions 32–38 choose the answer which you think fits best. Give one answer only to each question. You will hear the recording twice.

S: So, um, what do you do?

C: Well, I work as a casual sub-editor on the finance desk of *The Australian* newspaper. That's the only national daily in Australia. [Uh huh] It's one of the Murdoch newspapers. And, er ...

S: What does "casual" mean?

C: Well, it means I'm not one, part of the full-time staff. Quite a big proportion of the sub-editing staff on newspapers, certainly here, and I think in England as well, are casual employees who work two, three days a week. Some of them work on more than one newspaper, perhaps do double shifts. If you work on an afternoon paper like *The Mirror*, you'd start early in the morning and then you could go straight over to work on a morning paper like *The Australian* just about when your *Mirror* shift finishes. I mean, it's very hard work but some people do do that if they need to earn some money.

So how often do you do it?

I've just been doing three days a week. I resist all blandishments to do more because, well because I don't like to do too much of one thing.

And, um, tell me how it goes, from the moment you arrive. What happens?

Well, I don't know if you know what sub-editors do? Not everyone does. People often assume that you're sort of the deputy editor, which is a quite different thing. But sub-editors get the "copy", the story, into shape: correct grammar, spelling. Sometimes, depending on the sort of paper you're working on and the sort of reporter you're working on, rewrite stories if the reporter's not picked the best angle or the most newsy angle, or if you're told to take a different angle. Then you'll move that angle, that information up to the "intro", the first paragraph, and rewrite it from there. Um, you write the headlines, captions for pictures, "breakout heads", that's, you know, the little headlines that you get in the middle of the body of the copy and all that sort of thing.

What's the purpose of those?

The purpose, really, is just to break up the appearance of the page. If you get, even on a quality like *The Times* or *The Australian* , if you get a solid grey mass of copy, of type, people are deterred from reading it. It breaks it up into what looks like bite-sized pieces. The whole business of laying out a page, which is done also by sub editors called "layout subs", the whole business of laying out a page is to do with encouraging people to write, to read it. As indeed is the business of writing headlines and putting pictures in and all that.

So over the period of time how long do you spend in, on an evening doing it?

You do a full shift ...

Which is how long?

Which is about seven hours (OK) all told.

So how does the work, um, go over seven hours? Are there periods of boredom and inactivity?

There have been in the past but working on the finance desk now on *The Australian*, they've increased the size of "the book", the section, the finance section. And we now have a lot of foreign stories. Now because the Murdoch Press owns, say, *The Times* and various newspapers and magazines all over the world, we get a lot of stuff from other in-house publications. So, they, we work on those first off. We do the foreign pages of our section first off, you get stuff from *The Economist*, stuff from *The Washington Post*, all sorts of foreign copy. So we'll start at three o'clock in the afternoon, working on stuff from overseas and then we'll work towards the front of our section which will be, I mean, the main front pages will all be Australian stories. And they'll be coming in seven o'clock, eight o'clock, up to, say, about nine thirty deadline for the first edition. And then, once the first edition pages are done, we read them, between editions, correct any errors because we don't have a spell-check programme. It's quite primitive technology. Funnily enough, News Limited in Sydney was, if not the first, among the first newspapers in the world to be set up with what's called the new technology, electronic photo typesetting and all the rest of it. But it still has its original equipment from 1977 or something like that, so it's not, it's no longer state of the art, I need hardly say. Often there are areas that are not filled in the first edition, say in the third page or the fourth page, where we put in "house ads", what are called house ads, and that just means we advertise our own newspaper, you know, we say "Read Saturday's *Australian* for the property section" or, you know, something along those lines, or "Automotive business every Tuesday" or "Aviation on Wednesday afternoons," you know. And then we'll take the house ads out, with late breaking stories or with late comment from our own correspondents and replace those with stories.

Is it, is it satisfying to see your headlines in the paper the next day?

It is if they're good. Yes, yeah, If you've written a good one, if you've come up with something really nice. But surprising how rarely that happens on a po-faced paper like *The Australian* because they won't let you go in for all the jokes and the slang that you can use in a tabloid. So they have to be fairly high-brow jokes, you know, they have to be a bit sly.

Now you will hear the piece again.
That is the end of Section C.

Section D

You will hear five people talking about publications they read. Task one. Letters A–H list different types of publications. As you listen, decide which one on the list each speaker is referring to. For questions 39–43 put the letter of the publication against the appropriate speaker. Task two. Letters A–H list some of the positive features of the different publications which the speakers mention. As you listen indicate which two features are mentioned by each speaker. You will hear the recording twice.

The main point is that it helps you plan your viewing, obviously. But actually, there's a surprising amount in it besides programme listings. Articles about the soap stars, background to some of the popular series – quite interesting some of them, sometimes. And I especially like the competitions, puzzles, that sort of thing. It's not bad for 60p, is it? Cheaper than a lot of other glossy mags.

I wouldn't say it made riveting reading, but it's useful. I mean, you have to keep in touch with what's going on in your field. They have short pieces about new developments which are quite interesting and I always like to have a look at the job ads in case there's anything tempting. I wouldn't go out and buy it, no. But as it doesn't cost me anything as a union member, I'll give it a read.

I used to buy a paper everyday but not anymore. They take up such a lot of time, don't they? And you get all the important news on the telly

anyway. Now I just buy one on Sunday. It makes sense because you tend to get more in-depth articles, articles which look at the news in more detail, I mean, and there's more time to really read and enjoy them at the weekend. Oh, and I wouldn't want to miss the sports pages, of course.

It often comes with a free gift like a CD or a gadget for the hi-fi sytem, and that's fun. But what I particularly like about it is that every month they feature a different composer and go into a lot of detail about their life and their work and so on. We didn't do that sort of thing at school, so it's a way of educating myself. It costs £3.00, but there's so much in it, and the back numbers build up into a kind of reference book, of course, so I think it's well worth the price.

Most of it's rubbish, yeah. Loads of ads and boring stories about some school pupil winning a prize or some old couple's 50th wedding anniversary. A waste of money really. Still, I like to get the football results because I support a couple of local teams, and I also like the small ads. I got a really good second-hand fridge that way, and before that a bike, I remember.

Now you will hear the piece again.
That is the end of the test.

Test 3

Section A

You will hear some information about places to visit in the historic harbour area of the City of Bristol. For questions 1–11 complete the table by filling in the missing information. You will hear the recording twice.

Welcome to Bristol's historic harbour area. In the eighteenth century, Bristol was the leading English city and port outside London. Nowadays, the harbour is no longer used for commercial shipping and it has been redeveloped as a centre for leisure activities and water sports. As you walk around, however, you will see evidence of the harbour's history in the many waterside buildings.

One example close to the city centre is the Watershed. In Victorian times this was used as a storage shed but it has now been imaginatively redeveloped as a media centre with two cinemas, a gallery, and photographic studios.

A little further on, you'll find a boat called the Lochiel moored next to the quay. This was once a mail boat which was used to carry letters and packages in Scottish waters. The Lochiel has now been converted into a floating restaurant and it specialises in seafood.

Almost opposite the Lochiel is the Arnolfini. Now an important arts centre, which is well-known for its exhibitions of modern art, but in the last century it was a tea warehouse.

A few minutes' walk from the Arnolfini is the Thekla, another old boat which has found a new use. This was once a freight steamer but it's been converted into an entertainment centre with a very varied programme of entertainment ranging from jazz and rock to serious theatre and musicals. A favourite haunt for some of Bristol's 22,000 students.

There are many other places of interest if you continue your walk along the harbourside but the star attraction has to be the SS Great Britain, the world's first ocean-going ship to be built of iron, designed by the great engineer, Isambard Kingdom Brunel, and launched in 1843. The ship is now being restored in the very dry dock where she was built and is an important tourist attraction.

On the opposite side of the harbour, you'll find the Pump House, which is a popular restaurant nowadays. In times gone by it was the main pumping station for the harbour.

For an easy and very enjoyable way of seeing the harbour, why not take a water tour? The Bristol Packet was originally a working narrowboat carrying coal in the north of England. Now it's a pleasure boat offering tours of the harbour and beyond.

Now you will hear the piece again.
That is the end of Section A.

Section B

You will hear the details of a recipe. As you listen you must fill in the information for questions 12–19. Listen very carefully as you will hear the recording only once.

Today's recipe is for a delicious tomato and artichoke salad. It's very healthy – low in fat, high in fibre – and extremely quick and easy to prepare. Now for the details, and you can also find them on page 108 of Teletext.

You'll need 450 grammes of ripe tomatoes – make sure to test them for ripeness when you buy them. A 400 gramme can of artichoke hearts. A small onion – one of about 50 grammes should do. One large clove of garlic. 20 millilitres of lemon juice – that's about three teaspoons. 45 millilitres of olive oil – that's about three tablespoons. Make sure you use proper olive oil rather than a cheaper vegetable variety. 30 millilitres of fromage frais, which you can find in most supermarkets these days. Salt and pepper to taste and some fresh sprigs of basil.

Now the method: First of all, you'll need to drain the artichoke hearts. When you've removed all the liquid, cut them in half. Next, quarter your tomatoes. So, when the main ingredients are prepared, arrange everything on a suitable serving dish.

To make the dressing, first you'll need to roughly chop the onion. Then crush the garlic and put it, together with the lemon juice, the oil, the fromage frais and the seasoning, into a bowl. Use a whisk to blend together well. Once that's done, stir in the onion.

Finally, spoon the dressing over the prepared vegetables and the basil. Then cover and chill for about 30 minutes.

These ingredients are sufficient for four people and, at only 110 calories per portion, it's a dish which should appeal to most slimmers. The salad should be prepared shortly before serving and it is not suitable for freezing.

That is the end of Section B.

Section C

You will hear some advice about interviews. For questions 20–29 complete the sentences with an appropriate word or short phrase. You will hear the piece twice.

Interviewer: Have you got any tips that you could give me about interview techniques?

Brendan: Sure, well probably the most important thing is to make sure you get to the interview first. And that depends on putting in a good application, putting in a good curriculum vitae and a covering letter. Now there are two approaches to this. One is to have a very detailed curriculum vitae and a brief letter, or vice versa, having a very detailed letter and a very very brief curriculum vitae. It depends which system you're used to. So that's probably the most important step. Hopefully, that will get you an interview.

Now, from experience, I think the most important thing for an interview is to prepare properly, to make notes. Not to just turn up to the interview and answer questions. I think that's a big mistake people make. They go in there without any clear idea of what they want to get across or what they want to tell the interviewers. If you do that, it will be a one-sided interview, you will answer questions and that will be it. If you prepare, and you think of the different subject areas that you think you have expertise in, and the different experiences that you've had that you want to get across to the interviewers. You can make little brief notes about that. And somehow or other, when you're asked the questions, incorporate the information into your answers.

That way you have a little bit more control over the interview.

I know myself, having performed badly in a couple of interviews, I made that mistake. And it wasn't until later I realised I just answered the questions. They asked me a question, I answered the questions. I said nothing. I think the important thing with an interview is to use their questions as a springboard, as a platform for you to talk about yourself. And that also, incidentally, takes the pressure off them because they can sit back and they can listen to you. Because that's basically why they're asking questions. They want to find out about you. So it's always, it's a fine line between not appearing to be a high pressure salesman or saleswoman, in other words telling people how good you are, and just being confident. It's that balancing act between the two?

Interviewer: What about your, what you choose to wear on the big day? Is that important?

Brendan: I think it is, yeah. I think it's important to dress properly. You don't have to wear a suit. Not so long as you've got nice clothes. I think I would wear a suit or a nice shirt with a tie and stuff like that. But be aware of your dress. Don't turn up in what you do the gardening in, for example. Be aware and make sure you're properly presented because that definitely makes a difference, especially if you're going to a job in which you have to deal with a lot of people because they're looking for that.

Interviewer: And if you're the kind of person who feels uncomfortable in a suit, it's probably best not to, would you say?

Brendan: Yes, if it's going to make you feel uncomfortable, that would probably mean you don't perform well in the interview and that's a key point. An interview is a performance, that's what I think anyway. It's definitely a performance and if that makes you feel uncomfortable, you won't perform well, and you won't get the job. There are varying degrees of just how well you can dress. The old days, it was either a suit or nothing else, are gone. You can look very, very smart without wearing a suit. Nice shirt, nice jumper, good pair of trousers, etcetera, etcetera.

Now you will hear the piece again.
That is the end of Section C.

Section D

You will hear five different people talking about difficult interview experiences. Task one. Letters A–E list the different interview results. Decide which one on the list applies in each case. For questions 30–34 put the letter of the result against the appropriate speaker. A letter may need to be used more than once. Task two. Letters A–H list different problems which the interviewees may have had. For questions 35–39 put the letter of the problem against the appropriate interview. Letters may be used more than once. You will hear the recording twice.

My first interview I had as a teacher. I didn't get the job, incidentally, so it was particularly tricky. They asked me a question, I remember the question too, they said: "Have you ever taught an advanced class?", and I said "No". And they said "Do you find that very daunting?" and I says "Absolutely!" I realise now that perhaps I could have said "Yes I do find it daunting but I also find it challenging and I would like to teach advanced classes because that's where a lot of interesting work would go on. " In other words, you can give the truth but you can qualify it.

And I went into another company and they gave me a whole set of questions to answer and, being in the trade for, you know, almost twenty years, you forget about all the academic side of it and you're just doing the work. If they showed, told me how to do it on rigging – no problem. But when I had to do Ohm's Law, that was another story. And I just looked at some of the questions and I froze, I didn't know what to do. But I, although I was offered the job, I didn't take it and I was given a better position in the other company.

So I sort of got in there, and my hair was all flat and I walked in the room, and I'm a pretty casual kind of person and there were just four people sitting there on very high-backed chairs and about five feet away was my chair. And I sat there and everything that I'd thought about that I was going to say and how I was going to answer the questions, I just answered totally wrong, because I was just honest. And I'm the sort of person that if I feel something then I kind of show it. So I couldn't cover it up. And they were asking me things about, um, why had I sort of been away, because I'd been working abroad for six months. And I was saying, "Oh, I love being abroad and I love travelling and then I thought "Oh, what am I saying? I'm not supposed to say that." So it all went wrong from there, and then when I get embarrassed I go really red and I could feel the redness crawling up my face ...

Well, the man who interviewed me was, um, pretty aggressive from the word go and there was a point when he suddenly said: "Spell the word "supersede". So I spelt it S-U-P-E-R-C-E-D-E. And he snorted and sort of pushed the dictionary across the tabletop and said "Look it up", and, in fact, I'd made a mistake with the spelling but it's a tricky word.. And then he said, "And you seriously think you can be a teacher?" So I said "Well, I can always check spelling. I know I can teach". Amazingly, I did get the job in the end. I didn't really feel like working with the man but I needed the money!

A friend, I remember a friend of mine telling me about an interview that he went for with a really big multi-national company. And he was terribly nervous and he was sitting with a whole panel of people interviewing him, firing questions at him. But gradually, they brought him a cup of coffee and some biscuits, and he began to relax a little bit as he realised that the interview was going quite well. And as he really got into his stride, he completely forgot where he was and he dunked his biscuit in the coffee. And then he was expanding on a point and he stretched out his arm to make the point and bits of biscuit flew over the whole of the interviewing panel. He didn't get the job.

Now you will hear the piece again.
That is the end of the test.

Test 4

Section A

You will hear some advice about preventing car crime. For questions 1–10 complete the table by filling in the missing information. You will hear the recording twice.

Speaker 1:
Car crime is now a problem that affects us all, no matter where we live. Car thefts and thefts from cars make up almost a third of all reported crime. And about one in four of the cars reported missing each year is never recovered.

Such statistics don't take account of the delay and inconvenience to you, the owner, if your car gets stolen. It can take a month or more before insurance claims are paid out, and if your car is returned to you, it may be badly damaged and in need of repair.

Of all crimes, car crime is probably the most preventable. Simple and inexpensive measures can make an enormous difference in reducing the risk of your car becoming the next crime statistic.
Keep your car safe!

Don't leave luggage and valuables on display. Take them with you or lock them in the boot out of sight. And never leave credit cards in the glove compartment.

Lock the doors every time you leave your car.

Etch an identification number, such as your registration number, on to all glassware: the windows, head lamps and sunroof. Thieves won't want the expense of replacing them.

Remove your ignition key even when your car is in the garage.

Put your aerial down when you park.

When you're choosing a radio cassette machine for the car, look for a security-coded model which won't work if somebody tampers with it. Or buy a machine which is specially designed so that it can be easily removed when you leave your car.

Lockable wheel nuts are a sensible protection for expensive alloy wheels.

If you have a lockable fuel cap, thieves will be forced to abandon your car when it runs out of petrol.

Never leave vehicle documents in your car. Your registration document, MOT and insurance certificate could help a thief to sell your car.

The safest place to park is your garage, if you have one. if you don't, choose your parking space carefully. A busy, well-lit area is the safest. Thieves don't want to risk being seen.

You can get more information on crime prevention of all kinds by asking at your local police station for the leaflet called *Practical Ways to Crack Crime.*

Speaker 2:
That was a public information announcement on behalf of the City Police.

Now you will hear the piece again.
That is the end of Section A.

Section B

You will hear about a number of auction sales on a telephone information service. As you listen you must fill in the information for questions 11–17. Listen very carefully as you will hear this piece only once.

You have telephoned the Lloyds 24 hour recorded information service for sales at our Billingsgate office, telephone number 071 543 2717. Opening hours at this location are Mondays to Fridays between 9 am and 5.30 pm. and on Sunday, if applicable for special viewing, between 12 and 4 pm.

The sales at our Billingsgate Complex for the week beginning Monday 1st March are as follows:

Tuesday the 2nd of March: Old Master paintings at 10.30 am in our large gallery.

Wednesday the 3rd of March: Silver and Jewellery at 11.00 am, also in our large gallery. The showpiece of this sale is a magnificent matching set of diamond bracelet, brooch and wristwatch by Cartier. There will be Sunday viewing for this sale.

Thursday the 4th of March: Books, Atlases and Maps at 11.30 am in the Green Room.

Monday the 8th of March, European Stamps at 2 pm in the Long Gallery. This sale includes several rare and important stamps with estimates ranging from £100 – £3,000.

Wednesday the 10th of March: Rock and Pop Memorabilia from the '50s and '60s at 10.00 am in the large gallery.

Tuesday the 16th of March: Furniture and clocks at 11.00 am and 2.30 pm. The sale includes a large collection of 19th century desks and bookcases.

Friday the 19th of March: Classic Cars at 9.30 am. To be held at Filton Airfield near Reading.

Thursday the 25th of March: Toys and Dolls at 2.30 pm in the Green Room. Includes a number of dolls houses dating from the beginning of the century. There'll be Sunday viewing for this sale.

Lloyds sales are open to the public and entrance is free. You are welcome to attend, whether you intend to buy or just want to watch. If you are thinking of buying, most sales are on view three days prior to the sale. Catalogues can be purchased at the saleroom or ordered by telephone on our special catalogue Hot Line (071 543 2021).

Thank you for phoning the Lloyd's auction information service.

That is the end of Section B.

Section C

You will hear part of a radio interview with a doctor on the subject of jet lag. For questions 18–28 complete the sentence with an appropriate word or short phrase. You will hear this piece twice.

Interviewer: Now let's turn to a problem connected with modern travel that gets mentioned quite a lot these days – jet lag. I looked it up in the dictionary before we came on the air and what the dictionary says is this: *a slight sense of confusion and tiredness that people experience after a long journey in an aeroplane, especially after arriving in a place where the time is different from the place they left.* I've got Doctor Lesley Blake here in the studio. Tell me, Lesley, does jet lag really exist or is it all in the mind.

Lesley Blake: Yes, I think it's certainly true to say that jet lag exists. Anybody who's done a long haul flight from, say, New York to Paris will know what we're talking about, anyway. The problem is that the circadian rhythms ...

Interviewer: Circadian rhythms?

Lesley Blake: Yes, these are body rhythms that tell us when to eat and when to sleep and so on. These rhythms are affected by environmental cues – things like clock hour and temperature and whether it's day or night.

Interviewer: So what are the symptoms?

Lesley Blake: Well, you tend to have problems sleeping – you may fall asleep exhausted but then you wake up again three hours later in the middle of the night and lie awake for hours. You'll probably find your eating patterns are disrupted so you have no appetite when everyone else is eating but you may be starving hungry at midnight! The biggest problem, probably, is that one's performance, both mentally and physically, will be below par.

Interviewer: So, it's not a good idea for a business executive to fly across the Atlantic for an important meeting and then go home ...?

Lesley Blake: No, not if he, or she, needs to be on top form. It may not be such a problem on a really flying visit where you don't really need to adapt to a new time zone – you're not there for long enough – but, generally speaking, recovering from jet lag normally takes about one day for each time zone that you've crossed. So, if you, you're going somewhere like Australia, you will need several days to recover before you're at peak efficiency again. And things like climate and even culture can make a difference to your recovery rate too. You may find it takes longer to adjust to things in Hong Kong, say, in summer than in Sydney in their winter.

Interviewer: And are there remedies, anything we can take to prevent the effects of jet lag?

Lesley Blake: Anyone who could invent a remedy would become a millionaire! There are a few products on the market which promise to cure jet lag but there's no evidence that they work. Some people recommend carefully adjusting your sleeping patterns during the days before you leave so that you get used to sleeping later or earlier, whichever is closer to the time zone you'll be going to. That may work but it's pretty impractical for most people. But there are a few simple things you can do which help. You can try to get some sleep on the aircraft, for example. It's also best to avoid heavy meals though that may be easier said than done – airlines do insist on waking you up to feed you at regular intervals, don't they?

Interviewer: Yes, they do, it's maddening – but it's a way of passing the time, I suppose.

Lesley Blake: On the whole, it's best to accept that you won't be feeling at your best for a while and to avoid important commitments for at least 24 hours after you arrive.

Interviewer: So, some sensible advice on dealing with jet lag there from Dr Lesley Blake. Thanks Lesley.

Now you will hear the piece again.
That is the end of Section C.

Section D

You will hear four different people talking about ways of avoiding jet lag when travelling long distance. Task one. Letters A–D list the subjects the different speakers mention. As you listen, complete the boxes 29–32 with the appropriate letter A–D. You may use a letter more than once. Task two. Letters E–I list other points the speakers mention. As you listen, complete the boxes 33–37 with the appropriate letter E–I. You may use a letter more than once. You will hear the recording twice.

Speaker 1: Some people seem to claim that there's no such thing as jet lag. I personally don't agree with them. I think there definitely is. I certainly suffer from jet lag when I go from, say Australia to Britain, which is constantly flying backwards into yesterday. I think that jet lag isn't nearly as bad coming the other way, when you're flying east all the time. So perhaps a way of dealing with jet lag would be always to fly east. But that's not very helpful. Certainly travelling is made much more simple and much easier if you remember to drink lots of water on aeroplanes, to try to sleep before you get on the plane, and not to try to do it when you're already exhausted. That certainly helps.

Speaker 2: And the other is, as soon as you get to your destination, try not to fall asleep or have a little rest. Try and get into the rhythms of the day as soon as you get there. So, even if you arrive there at 7 o'clock in the morning and haven't slept for 24 hours, try to go through the whole day without having a little nap or sleep, and then go to bed that evening. So you're getting into the rhythm. It's hard. I've failed a couple of times, but I find from experience that's the best way to do it.

Speaker 3: I guess it's on, it depends on each individual how they wish to treat it. I, when I fly, if I'm tired at the end of a trip, I go to sleep no matter what time it is. I just crash. But other people try to stay up and go to bed when the sun goes down. And get up when the sun comes up .... . You dehydrate on board the aircraft so it's advisable to take as much fluid as you possibly can, not alcoholic of course, but anything that's got plenty of sugar in it to build your stamina up. And try and eat reasonably balanced meals. No junk food.

Speaker 4: ... yes, certainly, it can be extremely tiring. There are times when I'm sitting up in the middle of the night trying to keep awake, wondering what on earth made me pick this career! ... I think the answer is that you at times have to force yourself to go to bed when you don't want to. And at other times you force yourself to get up when you don't want to – to make your body, sort of show your body who's boss, so that you get back into local time zone as quickly as possible.

Now you will hear the piece again.
That is the end of the test.

Test 5

Section A

You will hear an advertisement which mentions special savings on several items of household equipment. For questions 1–12 complete the table by filling in the missing information. You will hear the recording twice.

Today and for the next seven days Snappy Super Stores are having a million pound clear-out. With thousands of items reduced by up to fifty per cent, 9 months free credit, and a range of unrepeatable free gifts and special offers, this is the sale you simply can't afford to miss!

Here are just some of the bargains on offer:
A Calypso colour television, the latest model with a 51 centimetre screen

and remote control. Sale price £499 – a saving of £50. And that's not all. This magnificent television comes with a four year guarantee at no extra cost.

Is your video recorder becoming a bit of an antique? Buy a new Ajax video, with all the latest features including remote control and long play and you'll save £40. The sale price is £389 and we challenge you to find one on sale cheaper anywhere else. In addition, you'll get ten free video cassettes as our gift to you.

Fed up with washing up? Now's your chance to buy that dishwasher you've always wanted. The Dido Dish-o-matic takes twelve place settings comfortably and it costs an affordable £369. That's a saving of £10 on the recommended retail price. And that's not all. We're also offering a £50 cheque back. Ask at the store for details of this free cheque offer.

Next, save an incredible £150 on a new Olympus cooker. It has a double oven and a beautiful, easy-care ceramic hob. Sale price, just £649 and you'll have the chance to win a luxury cruise too – ask at the store for details of this very special offer.

If you're concerned about economy <u>and</u> saving the planet, you can do your bit by buying a Pandora Chest Freezer. The Pandora is a low-energy model so it cuts down on bills and saves precious resources. We're offering it at the amazing price of just £369 – a saving of £60. Buy a freezer in the sale and you'll walk away with a free digital watch as well.

Lastly, is your vacuum cleaner past its best? Have you been thinking of replacing it? Well, now's your chance. The Luna Luxmaster is the vacuum cleaner which came out top in a recent consumer survey and it has the advantage of having built-in tools so you won't need to find somewhere to store them. The price is a ridiculous £99, which is a saving of £15 on the normal price. And free with the Luna Luxmaster is a personal stereo.

See these and thousands of other bargains in a Snappy Super Store near you. But hurry while stocks last!

Now you will hear the piece again.
That is the end of Section A.

Section B

You will hear some advice on complaining about a holiday. As you listen, you must fill in the information for questions 13–19. Listen very carefully as you will hear this piece only once.

... That's the bargain holidays that have caught our eye this week. If you're interested in any of them, you'd better act quickly, though, because these special offers are likely to prove very popular.

Now, what do you do when your dream holiday turns out to be more of a nightmare? We look at how to deal with holiday complaints.

First of all, by far the best thing is to try and deal with any problems at the time, while you're still at the resort. So explain your complaint clearly to the company representative. He or she may well be able to sort out the problem there and then.

When you're packing, remember to take the brochure describing the holiday and also a copy of the booking form. They will provide evidence of what you've been promised, whether it's a sea view or an entertainment programme for the kids.

One very useful piece of equipment you'll have with you is a camera. Use it to take photos of what you're complaining about: the condition of your room, for example, or the busy main road just in front of the hotel.

Keep all receipts for anything you have to spend to overcome the problems and make a note of the names and addresses of any other dissatisfied holidaymakers. It will be harder for the company to ignore a complaint if it 's confirmed by several people.

Finally, make sure you fill in the tour operator's complaint form and give it

to the the representative. Keep a copy, too, for future reference.

After the holiday, write to the company as soon as possible – some companies have a time limit for complaints – and say how much compensation you are asking for. Work out the compensation by deciding how many days of your holiday were spoiled and then calculating what proportion that is of of the total cost of the holiday.

And, if you still don't get satisfaction, you can contact ABTA, the Association of British Travel Agents, which operates an independent arbitration scheme for a registration fee of around £30.

If you would like our free fact sheet on Holiday Complaints, write to: "Having a Lovely Time", Television House, London W2 X 4LW.

That is the end of Section B.

Section C

You will hear an interview with Mary Dallas, an archaeologist, whose work involves studying aboriginal sites in Australia. For questions 20–29 complete the sentences with an appropriate word or short phase. You will hear the piece twice.

Interviewer: Would you say that you enjoy your job?
Mary Dallas: Absolutely!
Interviewer: And what about it makes it so enjoyable?
Mary Dallas: It's enjoyable because it's a combination of being out in the field wandering around in the bush and having that wonderful outdoor type of life as well as sitting behind a desk and slogging away using your brain etc.
Interviewer: And how much time do you spend outside in the field?
Mary Dallas: About a third, I think, of what I do.
Interviewer: And two thirds following it up?
Mary Dallas: Sitting at a desk, yes, being intelligent.
Interviewer: And when you say "walking around in the field", what does that mean? Does it mean literally ...?
Mary Dallas: It does. Bush walking, bush walking in the .... I would have to be looking for aboriginal sites in places that hadn't been greatly disturbed before, either by farming or by suburbs, or residential or industrial, or whatever. So that I'm looking basically in places that haven't been – the bushland is generally intact. So it's going to be like a nice bush walk.
Interviewer: Do you go on your own, or how many people go?
Mary Dallas: Oh, usually on my own. It depends. It depends on, I suppose, how rough it's going to be or whether it's going to be dangerous to be on your own or ...
Interviewer: What would make it dangerous?
Mary Dallas: The ruggedness, I suppose, of the terrain, so that you would have reason to worry about breaking a leg or falling down a cliff and then being on your own at the bottom of it. No-one hearing you cry.
Interviewer: What about animals? Snakes?
Mary Dallas: Ah well you see, you tend ... I mean you can overestimate the dangers in the bush but generally speaking I might see a snake two or three times a year, in all that time. You do see dangerous ones, of course. But you don't ...
Interviewer: Which are the dangerous ones?
Mary Dallas: In Australia, well they'd be tiger snakes and brown snakes and taipans up north.
Interviewer: And have you always wanted to be an archaeologist?
Mary Dallas: Since I was thirteen. Isn't that wonderful? I was one of those people who have always wanted to be an archaeologist instead of the ones who said, "Gee, I wish I was one." I went out and did it.
Interviewer: And at thirteen, what made you want to be an archaeologist?
Mary Dallas: Oh in those days it was classical archaeology that I was much more interested in. I think I read a book on Troy and that was the end of that. However, by the time I got to university the academic programs at Sydney for archaeology consisted of classical

156

archaeology, which was the straight Greek and Roman and Egyptian and Mesopotamian, and there was also an anthropology department which dealt with aboriginal culture and that one was simply far more interesting, so I went that way and left Greece and Rome behind.

Interviewer: And what's the best preparation to be an archaeologist if you're at school, you're fifteen years old and you're interested in ...

Mary Dallas: Oh if I could do it all over again, how would I become a better one? I think I'd probably do a lot more geology and geomorphology and natural science subjects. And it was, in the degree at Sydney it was extremely difficult to do that because the degree is part of an Arts course and in those days, this is a hundred years ago we're talking about, the science subjects were separated out pretty well. And if you wanted to do a science subject, you pretty well had to do a separate degree along with your Arts one, so it was very difficult then.

Interviewer: And what about opportunities for women? Is it a field that it's difficult for women to get into?

Mary Dallas: Traditionally it was – just about the only people who enrolled in the degree courses were women. And that was because there were so few career opportunities and it was, I mean in other words if you wanted to make money you went off and did Law or you went off and did Medicine. And archaeology wasn't seen as anything other than an academic pursuit. And in fact anthropology at Sydney University, Anthropology 1 was known as Marriage 1 – there's one in every university, I'm sure. So that you went off to find your husband by doing Anthropology 1. So that women did, women did it as a, not so much as a career event but they, as soon as it became a lucrative profession in the consulting area, suddenly the field is full of young boys expecting to make their fame and fortune. But it's too late, you see. We have the market cornered! All us older women.

Now you will hear the piece again.
That is the end of Section C.

Section D

You will hear five callers on a radio phone-in programme talking about speeches they have heard. Task one. The callers heard the speeches on different occasions. Look at the occasions listed, A–H, and put them in the order in which you hear about them by filling in the boxes numbered 30–34. Task two. The callers were impressed by the speeches for different reasons. Look at the list of reasons A–H and put them in order by filling in the boxes labelled 35–39. You will hear the recording twice.

Martin: ...Yes, and the thing about this speech that the bridegroom was giving was that he did it completely off the cuff. It didn't seem to be a prepared speech at all. He just stood up and started speaking and he had all the guests' attention immediately because it was so natural and direct. Normally when people give speeches, they're looking down a lot of time, aren't they, reading sort of prompt cards? And, it's not so um, ...

Presenter: Well, let me just interrupt there, Martin, because I think the very best speakers often don't have their speech written out, do they, and that's what makes them so effective. Perhaps they just have wonderful memories.

Presenter: You've touched on a very important point, there, Jack.

Jack: And the other speech, can I go on? [Course you can] was given by a man that works with me, not a professional speaker or anything. And he gave a speech to about 400, 500 of our colleagues who'd gathered to say good-bye to our boss who was retiring. And Bill had the boss to a T, you know, the way he was talking about our old boss was exactly as the boss was. And it was funny and it was witty. We were rolling about! It was great, it really was.

Presenter: Mary from Highbury. Good morning.

Mary: Good morning Jackie. Yes, I belong to our local Women's Institute and we get all sorts of speakers at our meetings but one we had recently was superb. I forget what the title was now but she made her point by telling a story – all about a train journey she'd made and

everything that happened. I won't tell it now because it would take too long but it kept us all listening because she made it so interesting and we wanted to know what happened next and we didn't realise until the very end what the point, the moral, was. It was very effective.

Presenter: Now we'll go over to Brenda who's in Fishponds.

Brenda: Yes, hello. Years ago my eldest son went to a school where the head teacher had that ability to make a really moving speech. I'll never forget when he first went there, there was a meeting where the head addressed all the new children and their parents. And it's quite a big thing, isn't it, when your child makes these giant steps in their life. The speech was really touching and by the end of that little assembly I mean even the men in the audience were sniffing and snuffling into their handkerchiefs. I think the really good speakers are the ones who can lead you through various feelings – bring a tear to your eye and make you think as well.

Presenter: Tony from Tetherington, hello to you.

Tony: Good morning Jackie. I'm president of the Rotary Club [Yes] and one thing we're very anxious about is to encourage young people in the ability to speak in public. And therefore we hold a public speaking competition every year for schoolchildren of under 16. [Uh huh] And it's a source of wonder to me that these young people can get up and talk for ten minutes and do it so well. I can remember clearly one young man who spoke to us – it was something to do with workers' rights – and he was so fired with his very strong views that we could all see him as a future Secretary General of a trade union.

Presenter: Thank you, Tony, for that. And thank you to everyone else who rang in ....

Now you will hear the piece again.
That is the end of the test.

ANSWER KEY

PRACTICE TEST 2

Paper 1

First Text
Animals in Danger

1/2/3/4	A, B, E, G
5/6/7/8/9/10	A, B, C, D, F, G

11	F	17	E
12	D	18/19	C, G
13	F	20	A
14	A	21/22	F, G
15	C	23	C
16	G	24	A

Second Text
Is the office fit for the job?

25	A	27	C	29	D
26	B	28	D	30	C

Third Text
Back-chat

31	F	33	G	35	D
32	A	34	B	36	C

Fourth Text
Letters

37	C	45	H
38	A	46/47	E, G
39	D	48	I
40/41/42	B, E, F		
43	A	49	K
44	J	50	G

Paper 3

Section A
1 Oscar's Winning Performance

0 D (example)

1	A	6	B	11	C
2	B	7	A	12	C
3	D	8	B	13	D
4	C	9	D	14	B
5	A	10	A	15	C

2 Cause for Alarm?

0 by (example)

16	in	23	apart
17	instead	24	as
18	Between	25	all
19	returning	26	will
20	Had	27	if
21	no one/nobody	28	so
22	what	29	in/within
		30	of

Section B
Homework

0 √ (example)
0 expenses (example)

31	wasted	39	clients
32	specially	40	√
33	reference	41	√
34	√	42	women
35	facilities	43	efficient
36	√	44	filing
37	computer	45	entire
38	establish	46	hardly

4 Photography Competition

0 winner (example)

47	judged
48	experts
49	appear/be printed/be published
50	value
51	closing date/final date/deadline
52	minimum
53	complete/fill in
54	returned
55	accompanied
56	a suitable/an appropriate
57	announced/published/printed
58	edition
59	responsibility

Section C
5 Car Chaos

0 F example

60	G	62	I	64	C
61	D	63	A	65	E

6 New Zealand

Answers should be marked according to 0–1–2 scale:

2 acceptable response linking the ideas successfully, with only minor errors.

1 response successfully communicates the information required, but with major error(s).

0 response communicates the wrong information and/or errors seriously impede intelligibility.

The following are example answers. Other versions are possible and marks should be awarded as appropriate.

66 The Maori name for New Zealand is Aotearoa, which means "Land of the Long White Cloud".

67 The North Island, where most of the people live, has fertile plains, mountain ranges and a volcanic region with several active volcanoes.

68 In the South Island, the Southern Alps form an unbroken chain 650 kilometres long and reach their highest point in Mount Cook, which is 3704 metres high.

69 The country has a population of 3.3 million and the languages spoken are English, the official language, and Maori.

70 The capital is Wellington, known as the "Windy City", which is a port in the southern part of the North Island.

71 The climate is cool and temperate with a maximum temperature of 24°C in January/February and a minimum temperature of 6°C in July.

72 The country's main exports are dairy products, wool, mutton and lamb, while tourism is also an important source of income.

Paper 4

Section A
Answering Machines

1	15	9	√	17	√
2	120	10	√	18	√
3	60	11	√	19	X
4	150	12	X	20	√
5	X	13	√	21	√
6	√	14	X	22	√
7	X	15	X	23	X
8	√	16	√		

Petra

24	Sally Taylor/Tailor
25	sandwiches and fruit
26	by (the) swimming pool
27	(the) gold market
28	musical entertainment
29	comfortable clothing/clothes
30	(a) Turkish fort
31	(the) hotel lobby

Section C
Sub-editor

32	C	35	D	37	C
33	B	36	B	38	A
34	D				

Section D
Publications

39	F	44	D	49	F
40	E	45	A	50	A
41	H	46	E	51	H
42	D	47	B	52	E
43	A	48	H	53	F

PRACTICE TEST 3

Paper 1

First Text
Cruising

1	C	7/8	C, E	15	B
2	B	9	A	16	E
3	E	10	E	17/18	C, E
4	A	11	D	19	A
5	D	12/13	A, B		
6	A	14	D	20	E

Second Text
Prince of Wales

21	G	23	A	25	B
22	D	24	F	26	C

Third Text
Classrooms with the writing on the wall

27	D	29	A	31	C
28	B	30	C	32	B

Fourth Text
How to win prizes for keeping quiet

33	D
34/35/36/37	C, G, H, K
38/39	I, J
40	E
41/42	B, F
43	K
44	C
45	H
46	E
47	K
48/49/50	A, C, J
51	A

Paper 2

See notes on marking and assessment criteria on page 11.

Paper 3

Section A
1 Talking rubbish

0 B (example)

1	B	6	B	11	A
2	C	7	D	12	B
3	A	8	C	13	C
4	C	9	A	14	A
5	D	10	D	15	D

2 New £20 note to prevent forgeries

0 has (example)

16	the/any
17	being
18	in
19	Anyone
20	could
21	be
22	across/over
23	with/to
24	into
25	make
26	seen/read/detected
27	on
28	with
29	Each/Every
30	of

Section B
3 Travel free as an air courier

0 √ (example)
0 travel? (example)

31 √

32 fee.
33 price?
34 √
35 airlines.
36 yourself?
37 √
38 distributors.
39 rewarding.
40 living.
41 √
42 often.
43 all.
44 √
45 savings.

4

0 regret (example)
46 unable
47 attend
48 be held/take place
49 matters/business/affairs
50 agreed/offered
51 place
52 report
53 opportunity
54 support/agree with
55 raise/increase
56 seems to/appears to
57 result in/lead to
58 reduction/decrease
59 in favour
60 introduce/impose

5 Book reading a lost art at Harvard

0 H (example
61 F   63 A   65 G
62 J   64 C   66 E

6 Stretching Exercises

Answers should be marked according to a 0–1–2 scale:

2 acceptable response linking the ideas successfully, with only minor errors.

1 response successfully communicates the information required, but with major error(s).

0 response communicates the wrong information and/or errors seriously impede intelligibility.

The following are sample answers. Other versions are possible and marks should be awarded as appropriate.

67 Place your heels firmly on the floor and lean forwards with your hands resting on the wall so that your calf muscles are slightly stretched.

68 Hold this position for 30 seconds and then lean further for a little extra stretch.

69 Stand with your feet wide apart and lean forwards so

that you are pushing the palms of your hands towards the floor,

70 Hold this position for 30 seconds, as before, remaining relaxed and breathing calmly.

71 With your left foot forward and your right food back behind you, bend your left leg, keeping your back straight.

72 Standing on your right leg, grasp your left ankle with your left hand and pull it up until you feel a stretch in the front of your thigh.

73 Repeat the exercise with the other leg.

Paper 4

Section A
Bristol Harbour

1 storage shed
2 media centre
3 mail boat
4 (floating) restaurant
5 tea warehouse
6 arts centre
7 entertainment centre
8 tourist attraction
9 pumping station
10 restaurant
11 pleasure boat

Section B
Recipe

12 ripe
13 olive oil
14 Drain
15 Quarter
16 Roughly chop
17 Stir in
18 Cover and chill
19 for freezing

Section C
Interviews

20 application
21 very detailed
22 brief
23 making notes
24 one-sided
25 control over
26 springboard/platform
27 pressure
28 your dress
29 perform well

Section D
Interviews

30 C   34 C   37 C
31 A   35 D   38 F
32 E   36 H   39 A
33 B

PRACTICE TEST 4

Paper 1

First Text
How to find out about dinosaurs

1 G   8/9 A, F   16 E
2/3 D, F 10 B   17 F
4 C   11 H   18 G
5 D   12 I   19 A
6 H   13 B
7 B   14/15 A, I

Second Text
Healthier way of life underground

20 D   22 G   24 A
21 B   23 E   25 C

Third Text
Curing the ill-mannered

26 D   28 C   30 A
27 B   29 C   31 B

Fourth Text
Looking for the special agents

32 F
33/34 C, D
35/36 A, B
37 C
38 E
39 B
40 A
41/42/43 A, B, E
44/45 D, F
46/47 A, E
48 F
49 D

Paper 2

See notes on marking and assessment criteria on page 11.

Paper 3

Section A
1 Hotels pick up bills for five-star thieves

0 C (example)

1 B   6 B   11 D
2 D   7 C   12 C
3 A   8 B   13 B
4 A   9 D   14 A
5 C   10 A   15 D

2 Forest Fires

0 each/every (examples)
16 where
17 Anyone/Someone
18 to   23 seems/appears
19 (in)to   24 As/while
20 So   25 for
21 being   26 up
22 can   27 (in)to
              28 Yet/However/But
              29 if
              30 our

Section B
3 Flu takes area by storm

0 has descended (example)
0 √ (example)

31 were jammed
32 deal
33 has been
34 √
35 buying
36 √
37 was trying
38 wouldn't feel
39 √
40 have
41 have seen
42 √
43 were cancelling/ had cancelled
44 feel
45 recommends

4

0 aged between (example)
46 spare
47 the weekends
48 meeting/talking to
49 earn
50 looking for
51 dishes
52 a hand
53 from time
54 head
55 four-hour
56 whichever (one)
57 any tips
58 below

Section C
5 Health Advice for Travellers

0 K (example)
59 L   62 E   65 I
60 H   63 A   66 G
61 B   64 D

6 James Joyce

Answers should be marked according to a 0–1–2 scale:

2 acceptable response linking the ideas successfully, with only minor errors.

1 response successfully communicates the information required, but with major error(s).

0 response communicates the wrong information and/or errors seriously impede intelligibility.

Sample Answers

67 He was educated at Belvedere College and later at (a) university in Dublin, where he studied philosophy and also took an interest in the theatre.

68 He left Ireland in 1904, already convinced of his destiny as a great writer, going first to Zurich and then to Trieste, where he earned a living by teaching English.

69 By 1904 he had completed a collection of short stories called *Dubliners* but

problems with his publishers prevented its publication for ten years.

70 His first novel, *A Portrait of an Artist as a Young Man*, published in 1916, was immediately recognised as a masterpiece and received many enthusiastic reviews.

71 In 1922, his most famous novel, *Ulysses,* which had been written over a period of seven years, and gave a very detailed description of a day in the lives of various Dubliners, was published in France.

72 He lived in Paris after 1920, and despite poor eyesight which made it necessary for him to use his friends as readers and secretaries, he completed his last work, *Finnegan's Wake*, two years before his death in 1941.

Paper 4

Section A
Keep your Car Secure
1 inconvenience
2 preventable
3 on display
4 credit cards
5 an identification/ your registration
6 in the garage
7 easily removed
8 abandon
9 sell your car
10 well-lit

Section B
Auctions
11 12–4pm
12 Silver and Jewellery
13 European Stamps
14 Furniture and Clocks
15 Toys and Dolls
16 three days
17 Catalogues

Section C
Jet lag discussion
18 confusion
19 tiredness
20 temperature
21 sleeping
22 performance
23 time zone
24 climate
25 no evidence
26 (get some) sleep
27 (eating) heavy
28 (at least) 24 hours

Section D
Jet Lag excerpts
29 B 32 A 35 I
30 A 33 G 36 E
31 D 34 H 37 H

PRACTICE TEST 5

Paper 1

First Text
Fire Extinguishers
1 A 4 B
2 D 5 B
3 C 6 D
7/8 A, B
9/10 B, C
11/12/13/14 B, D, E, F
15/16 C, E
17 F
18/19/20 B, C, E
20/21/22 B, C, E
24 D

Second Text
High-tech teaching practice
25 B 28 A 31 C
26 A 29 D 32 C
27 D 30 B 33 B

Third Text
Why Aborigines are speaking Portuguese
34 F 36 G 38 C
35 B 37 A 39 E

Fourth Text
Service without a smile
40 F 44 A 48 F
41 D 45 E 49 E
42 F 46 F 50 B
43 C 47 D

Paper 2

See notes on marking and assessment criteria on page 11.

Paper 3

Section A
1 Flying Pigeons Forever
0 D (example)
1 C 6 C 11 A
2 B 7 A 12 B
3 A 8 B 13 D
4 B 9 C 14 C
5 D 10 D 15 C

2 Skiing at the limits
0 in (example)
16 In/Within
17 All 22 will
18 without 23 held
19 to 24 for
20 goes 25 like
21 for 26 both
27 But/However
28 on
29 by
30 can/could/may/might

Section B
3 How to have a baby and save your career
0 to (example)
0 with (example)

0 √ (example)
31 the
32 to
33 √
34 while
35 √
36 who
37 if
38 not
39 √
40 than
41 to
42 √
43 of
44 be
45 √
46 will

4 Top Floor Flat
0 moved into (example)
47 inform you
48 attention
49 inspected/visited
50 behalf
51 aware/informed/told
52 pointed
53 important/urgent/pressing
54 leak
55 safety/health
56 replacing/mending
57 cleaning
58 constantly
59 undertake/do/organise
60 delay
61 alternative

Section C
5 Adapting to the climate
0 G (example)
62 F 64 I 66 A
63 C 65 D

6 TOUR TS 1215
Answers should be marked according to a 0–1–2 scale:
2 acceptable response linking the ideas successfully, with only minor errors.
1 response successfully communicates the information required, but with major error(s).
0 response communicates the wrong information and/or errors seriously impede intelligibility.

Sample Answers
0 Please report to the Skyways check-in desk in Terminal 3 at least 2 hours before departure time.
67 Please ensure that each piece of luggage carries the Skyways label clearly marked with your name and address in block capitals.
68 The Skyways Airbus departs at 10.25 am and a light lunch will be served during the 2 hour 10 minute flight.
69 After a welcome reception at the airport, coaches will depart for the short drive to the Concorde Hotel where 7 nights' accommodation has been booked.
70 While films are available at the hotel, the choice is very limited so we suggest you

purchase films before travel, and the same applies if your camera needs batteries.
71 For the daytime, light clothing in natural fibres is recommended and, for evening wear, smart casual clothing, but not shorts or swimwear, would be suitable.
72 There will be free time for shopping on Thursday and Saturday, and our travel representatives will advise on the best places to go and the best bargains to look for.
73 Tips are included for all the meals in the tour but not for the guides or bus drivers, for whom we would suggest a maximum of 12 dollars each at the end of the tour.

Paper 4

Section A
Great Savings!
1 screen
2 four-year guarantee
3 long play
4 £389
5 Dishwasher
6 £50 cheque back
7 double oven
8 free cruise
9 low energy
10 £60
11 Vacuum cleaner
12 personal stereo

Section B
Holiday Complaints
13 representative
14 booking form
15 Take photos/pictures
16 receipts
17 complaint(s) form
18 compensation
19 registration fee

Section C
Archaelologist
20 behind/at a desk
21 a third
22 farming
23 dangerous
24 breaking a leg
25 snakes
26 thirteen
27 at university
28 (natural) science
29 men/(young) boys

Section D
Speeches
30 D 34 E 37 D
31 F 35 F 38 E
32 A 36 A 39 B
33 H